Researching into Student Learning and Support
In Colleges and Universities

**MARGARET JONES, JOHN SIRAJ-BLATCHFORD
AND KATE ASHCROFT**

**KOGAN
PAGE**

London • Stirling (USA)

First published in 1997

Kogan Page Limited
120 Pentonville Road
London N1 9JN
and
22883 Quicksilver Drive
Stirling, VA 20166, USA

© Margaret Jones, John Siraj-Blatchford and Kate Ashcroft, 1997

British Library Cataloguing in Publication Data

A CIP record for this book is available from the British Library.

ISBN 0 7494 1772 2

Typeset by Kogan Page
Printed and bound in Great Britain by Clays Ltd, St Ives plc

Contents

CONTENTS

List of Research Tasks

Chapter 2

Investigating student concerns
Annotated bibliography
Interviews: evaluation of an institutional issue
Course evaluation
Action research: evaluation formats

Chapter 3

Investigating the counselling role
Questionnaire survey: students' experience in relation to
   accommodation
Interviews: students' financial problems
Comparative study: institutional cooperation and competition
Document analysis: investigating the operation of the Access Fund
Individual and group interviews: investigating the communication
   systems for student help

Chapter 4

Focus group techniques: special consideration groups
Group interviews: parental involvement in the education of students
   with disabilities
Document search and interviews: course materials
Questionnaire: comparison of male and female job opportunities
Comparison of socio-economic categories for differing institutions
Comparison of provision for gay, bisexual and lesbian students
Student representation and the workings of committees
Semi-structured interviews: representation from students' perspectives

Chapter 5

Ideological deconstruction
Symbolic interactionism

Chapter 1
Series Introduction
Kate Ashcroft

The research that colleges and universities engage in covers a very wide spectrum, including basic research into fundamental problems as well as entrepreneurial work, often contracted by a particular customer. Each of the books in this series is focused on a particular form of research: that of small-scale insider research. Each looks at issues of teaching, learning and management within colleges and universities from the point of view of the novice researcher. The aim is to provide you with starting points for research that will help you understand and improve your practice, that of your students and the context for learning and teaching that your institution provides. The research that you undertake may also help you to understand the context in which teaching and learning is managed, and should provide you with the raw material for publication in research-based media.

The series is aimed at creating a range of quick and easy to read handbooks, so you can get started on research into aspects of your practice. Each book includes a version of this introductory chapter by the series editor about insider research, its principles and methods. If you have read the series introduction in another of the books in the series, you may wish to skip parts of this chapter and go straight to the section *Main issues and topics covered in this book* towards the end of this chapter.

Each book in the series also includes a concluding chapter by the series editor that provides guidelines on writing for publication and information about publishing outlets, including an annotated list of publishers and journals interested in educational research in further and higher education in general and student learning and support in particular.

The chapters in this book are focused on contemporary issues. They include a range of examples of research instruments and suggestions as to how you might use or adapt them to your own context for enquiry. The starting points for research cover the following areas:

- the perspectives of the main participants in the educational process;
- the context in which they operate;
- their existing practice;
- their existing values; and
- the relationships between the context and the values and practice.

A range of methods used in insider research in education is included within the research tasks.

This book provides an introduction to some of the issues in student support, located within a clear commitment to equality of opportunity. It cannot include sufficient information for you to complete a research project for publication. You will need to find out more about the subject matter and the research methodology that you decide to use. Similarly, the books will introduce you to some of the theoretical frameworks open to you, but the discussion will not be deep enough, of itself, to ensure that your research is 'grounded in theory'. For these reasons, a list of additional reading is included at the end of the chapters.

The books in the series should appeal to lecturers in further and higher education who are interested in developing research skills and who would find concrete suggestions for research and some exemplar research questions and instruments helpful. For this reason, the authors have aimed for an accessible and readable style of writing. Care has been taken to keep sentences and paragraphs short and the writing practical, informal and personal. We have tried to avoid using technical terms and jargon unnecessarily, but where these have to be included, we have tried to explain them in as simple a way as possible.

Synopsis of the Series

This book is one of a series that includes the following books:

- *Researching into Assessment and Evaluation in Colleges and Universities* (Ashcroft and Palacio, 1996);
- *Researching into Teaching Methods in Colleges and Universities* (Bennett, Foreman-Peck and Higgins, 1996);
- *Researching into Student Learning and Support in Colleges and Universities* (Jones, Siraj-Blatchford and Ashcroft, 1997);
- *Researching into Learning Resources in Colleges and Universities* (Higgins, Reading and Taylor, 1996); and

- *Researching into Equal Opportunities in Colleges and Universities* (Ashcroft, Bigger and Coates, 1996).

The series aims to provide you with a framework of ideas and starting points for research which can be carried out alongside your current practice. The books present these ideas in such a way that, rather than detracting from your practice, they might enhance it. They introduce methods for you to use (adapted or not) for researching into your own teaching. Most of the ideas do not require visits outside of your institution and suggest data that could be available with a fairly modest outlay of energy.

You should find the books useful if you are new to teaching or if you are an experienced lecturer who needs or wishes to develop a research profile within education. In the case of higher education, this is a major focus that involves all tutors. You may be under pressure to publish for the first time in order to contribute to research rating exercises. You might be undertaking a qualification that includes a research element. A masters degree or doctorate is an increasing requirement for promotion in further and higher education. In the UK, more masters degree courses are being developed and geared towards this sector. In higher education, many staff are now expected to achieve a doctorate. Some of the starting points within this book could be developed into a fairly sophisticated research project.

You may be interested in researching your own practice for its own sake. For instance, you may wish to investigate self-advocacy approaches to curriculum design. The interest in insider research is percolating into colleges and universities from the action research movement within schools and may grow at a comparable rate.

Insider Research and the Model of Reflection

Insider research is a form of participant research. It is principally about understanding and improving practice within the researcher's institution. It can be focused on a problem and involve cycles of data collection, evaluation and reflection, in which case it is called action research. Carr and Kemmis (1986) provide an easy to read account of the process of action research. Other books in this series that take you step by step through the process are Bennett *et al.* (1996) and Ashcroft and Palacio (1996); it is also discussed in Chapter 2 of this book.

Insider research need not be problem-centred. It is an appropriate approach for a matter of personal curiosity or interest that you decide to investigate in a systematic way. Many tutors who have used the approach have found that insider research is an empowering process. It often comes up with surprises and enables you to see problems in new ways. It is probably the most effective way of exploring the functioning of real-life classrooms and investigating the effects of your interventions on student experience and learning. It deals with the real problems and issues you face and, in doing so, may transform those problems and the way you construe teaching and learning. It has a moral base, in that it allows you to explore your actions and those of others in the light of the values that supposedly underpin them.

If you are to be a successful insider researcher, you will need to identify a *critical @D Head* = group or community that will help you identify appropriate research questions, refine your research instruments and evaluate your reflections and data as you go along, and help you to ensure that you are considering ethical issues. When you are exploring issues of student support, this group may often be the students themselves. You will also need to seek alternative interpretations of your data from a number of sources and to read widely, in order to locate your insights in a wider context.

When I have engaged in this kind of research and publication, the key thing I have discovered is the need to relate my findings to a theoretical framework (see, for instance, Ashcroft and Griffiths, 1990 or Ashcroft and Peacock, 1993). Very occasionally, I have developed my own framework, but more usually I have used an existing one to analyse my findings. Without such analysis, the results of insider research tend to be anecdotal and descriptive.

The series is built on a theoretical framework provided by the reflective practitioner of education as described by Dewey (1916) and developed by Zeichner, Ashcroft and others (see, for instance, Ashcroft, 1987; Ashcroft and Griffiths, 1989; Deakin University, 1982; Isaac and Ashcroft, 1986; Stenhouse, 1979; Zeichner, 1982; Zeichner and Teitlebaum, 1982). The model takes the view that 'knowledge' is not absolute or static and that lecturers in further and higher education should take an active role in constructing, deconstructing and reconstructing it. We look at deconstruction particularly in Chapter 5 of this book. The process of action does not take place in a social or political vacuum. It is part of the lecturer's role to work collaboratively with others, particularly with students, to create morally and educationally justifiable solutions to problems. This is a continuing theme in this book.

This suggests that educationists have some sort of moral responsibility for their subjects and the processes of research, and that it is part of their duty to act as whistle-blowers when the powerful define truth in ways convenient for their purposes. It sees reflective practice as much more than a passive 'thinking about'. It embraces active professional development, directed at particular qualities: open-mindedness (a willingness to seek out and take account of the views of a variety of other people, particularly to give a voice to the least powerful student groups); commitment (a real and sustained attachment to the value of your work and to improving its content and the experience of students); and responsibility (a concern with the long- as well as the short-term consequences of action). The enquiry considers the question of 'What works?' but also moves on to pose questions of worthwhileness. This demands investigation into action, intervention and the perspectives of a number of the participants in the educational process: students, tutors, institutional managers, employers, funding agencies and community representatives. In this book, we focus particularly on the student as the major stakeholder in the education process. It also suggests that intentions, attitudes and values are explored, as well as behaviour and outcomes. Each of the qualities of open-mindedness, commitment and responsibility has particular definitions and prerequisite skills and understandings. Our intention in introducing you to the research process is to enable you to collect data and to analyse them in the light of your emerging theory of practice (see Argyris and Schon, 1974, for more details of this notion of theory in action).

This series of books is partially directed at helping you to acquire research skills and skills of analysis. For this reason, this book includes a variety of examples of ways to collect and organize data that you might use to find out about the behaviours, thoughts, attitudes and experience of students, other lecturers, managers, employers and others. This kind of research and data collection is particularly relevant to the development of open-mindedness.

Responsibility implies that you collect evidence as to your effectiveness and the intended and unintended outcomes of your teaching and management. We suggest a range of research instruments that may help you and your students discover what you actually do (as opposed to what you think you do) in the course of your and their work, what effects your behaviour has on others, how they see it and the attitudes resulting from it.

Commitment implies a real and sustained attachment to the value of your work and to improving its context. You need optimism in order to sustain this: to believe that you are one of the stakeholders in the institution and community, and that you have the duty and power to effect changes and to secure the appropriate teaching and learning environment for your students. This is not easy, particularly in circumstances where resources are very short or where you work within an autocratic or chaotic management regime. Insider research cannot solve these kinds of problems, but it may help you to understand their nature and go some way to helping you to cope.

In slightly more positive circumstances, insider research can be empowering. Empowerment of students is an important theme in this book. This kind of research is one way of finding out about the needs and interests of others, and expressing these in terms that create a powerful case for change. For this reason, we have included a range of starting points for research that will enable you to enquire into management issues and the working of your institution and the ways that they impact on students.

I have stated that research skills are an essential prerequisite to reflective practice. This should not be taken to mean that they are sufficient. Reflective practice in teaching also requires that you acquire a range of other skills. These include technical teaching skills, such as voice projection; interpersonal skills such as counselling skills and the ability to work as part of a team; communication skills in a variety of contexts; and the ability to criticize the status quo from a moral point of view. Insider research, perhaps uniquely, can help you to acquire each of these skills. By providing feedback on your actions, insider research directs you to problems that you are creating or failing to solve. You can then experiment with new ways of approaching them and use insider research to provide information on the effectiveness of your new ways of thinking and acting.

The elaborated form of this cycle of evaluation, action and data collection (action research) is a particularly potent form of research for developing reflective practice, especially if you test your interpretation of results in a variety of ways: for instance, through using a range of research methods to look at the same issues or by testing your interpretation of data against those of other parties to the educational process.

Nobody is able to sustain reflective practice at all times. During the process of teaching and research you may frame your problem according to assumptions that you feel comfortable with, you may interpret data to fit your preferred solution, or you may fail to notice the most important data. For this reason, we suggest that your methods and interpretation should be made public in some way.

Reflective practice requires that you question your deepest beliefs and compare your actions with your values. In doing this, you may find that you must abandon cherished beliefs or practices. Despite the loss that change brings and the risks that it involves, the value of reflective practice is in the process of continual questioning and renewal that is essential for professional development and growth in understanding.

Research in Colleges and Universities

An increasing number of people expect to be educated to at least degree level. For instance, in the UK, the proportion of young people going into higher education has doubled in recent years. When the members of this educated population enter colleges and universities, they expect to be taught by people who are expert at a very high level. This expertise is generally achieved through research and publication or through higher degree work that involves research. Education at this level is being seen as an increasingly rigorous process. Quality and standards in the sector have come under continuous scrutiny. One of the determinants in the assessment of quality is the level of expertise of staff. Staff who aspire to promotion may have to obtain higher level qualifications that include substantial research (Ashcroft and Foreman-Peck, 1995).

The growth of the pool of highly educated people means that there is increasing competition for permanent posts in colleges and universities. These posts usually go to those who can provide evidence that they are more 'expert' than their competitors. In the UK, the numbers of staff on fixed-term contracts in universities and colleges is growing. In the USA, a glut of highly educated professors means that the proportion of part-time staff in colleges and universities has doubled in the last 20 years (Irwin, 1995). The emphasis in universities on research ratings and the decision in many Western countries to make these public has created a 'publish or die' culture. University lecturers are expected to publish papers and books with increasing regularity. Where colleges aspire to include higher level courses within their portfolio, they often find that the staff who teach such courses are expected to demonstrate a research record that equals that of colleagues in the university sector.

Busy lecturers need to find a time-efficient way to research and publish. If you engage in insider research, you are likely to find your results are interesting and that they might have more general application. A number of my colleagues who engage in fairly small-scale research of this type, mainly for their own interest, have then published the resulting papers in refereed journals. For instance, I became interested in the process of developing criteria for the assessment of student teacher competence in classrooms. Discussions with colleagues and the collection of a variety of data led to the conclusion that the establishment of 'clear' criteria for the assessment of teaching was by no means a matter of creating a simple checklist of 'indicators of appropriate action'. My colleague and I were able to publish a paper outlining our small-scale study and conclusions in a refereed, international journal (Ashcroft and Tann, 1988).

In effect, I am suggesting 'quick and dirty' research as appropriate for the hard-working lecturer who wants to improve his or her practice. This can be somewhat refined and elaborated for publication. There is interest among editors and readers of journals in small-scale, modest research that focuses on the real dilemmas that lecturers face. On the other hand, insider research does have its weaknesses. In particular it is prone to self-justification and can be very inward-looking. I therefore suggest that, as for the development of reflective practice, if you are to be a successful insider researcher, you will need to identify a *critical* group or community to help you refine your research and to locate it within the research literature.

Research Rating

Research can be defined and rated in a variety of ways. For the purposes of this series, I am using the definition of research provided by the Higher Education Funding Council for England:

> Research... is... original investigation undertaken in order to gain knowledge and understanding. It includes work of direct relevance to the needs of commerce and industry, as well as to the public and voluntary sectors, scholarship; the invention and generation of ideas, images, performances and artefacts including design, where these lead to new or substantially improved insights; and the use of existing knowledge in experimental development to produce new or substantially improved materials, devices or processes, including design and construction.(HEFCE, 1994, p.7)

In the UK a system of research ratings linked to funding makes most lecturers in higher education very aware of the imperative to publish and establish a reputation in the world of research and scholarship. The HEFCE research rating exercise affects institutional funding and, if you work in higher education, it is important that you understand the 'rules of the game'. Unfortunately, these are not always explicit and stable. Education at this level is being seen as an increasingly rigorous process.

Quality and standards in the sector have come under continuous scrutiny. One of the determinants in the assessment of quality is the level of expertise of staff, including their research record.

Below I describe the system for rating research used in the UK. This is a fairly typical system. Research ratings in other counties will have similarities; some will also have important differences. For instance, the UK research rating exercise does not include any count of the number of times a person's work is cited in others' research.

Subject organizational units in higher education are invited to compete for research funding. (Subject organizational units often correspond to subject departments and so, in the interests of readability, I shall refer to them as 'departments' from now on.) The success of departments in generating funded research activity, recruiting research students, employing research staff and enabling individual staff to research and publish determines how much (if any) money is allocated to that institution for research activity. (Of course, if a department is successful, it does not follow that the institution must allocate all the funds it 'wins' to that particular department.) The rating also affects how the department is viewed by the managers of other research funds, potential students and other customers. A high rating may be taken as a rough and ready measure of the quality of research work within a department. It is likely to encourage potential investors to allocate funds to the department and students to apply to it.

The research activity of individual lecturers within a department is therefore an important aspect of the research rating exercise. Interestingly, the research and publication activity of individual lecturers is 'attached' to the individual, rather than the institution where the activity took place. This means that if you are an active researcher, you take your research and publication rating with you when you move job, and so research activity may be the key to your employability.

The operation of research rating exercises can be the subject of investigation in itself. For example, you might explore whether measures that can compare a large number of instances across a sector of education provide opportunities for manipulation by powerful or unscrupulous groups or individuals. Some of these influences might be hard to get at. For instance, the older, more prestigious universities can band together to lobby for measures that favour traditional forms of research or, in countries where the measures include 'citation counts', a group of researchers may operate a 'citation syndicate', each citing the work of the others whenever the opportunity arises.

Starting Points for Research: Values and Practice

We do not provide a total blueprint for research. This would be impossible, given the variety of contexts in which the readers of the series work and the variety of findings they are likely to come up with. Even if it were possible to lay out a complete research project for you to follow, we would not wish to do so. A large part of the new knowledge and understanding gained from research comes from the stimulus to creativity that asking your own questions and looking at preliminary data provide. In collecting your own data and then asking questions of yourself such as, 'What do I need to know to interpret these data?', 'How can I get at the meanings behind these data?' or, 'What other data do I need?', you will come up with transformational resolutions to research questions that are far more innovative and creative than any the authors could suggest. Therefore, you should feel free to interpret research tasks widely: to adapt and alter suggested foci for research and ideas for data collection to fit your own context and, most importantly, to go beyond the first cycle of data collection to ask your own questions.

It is important to be aware of the limitations of small-scale research. If you claim a spurious objectivity to your work, you are likely to miss the most important strength of insider research: the opportunity it offers to you to explore your existing practice and that of others, the stated values that underpin this practice and the relationship between those values and the practice. 'Practice' may seem to you to be the most objective of these elements but, in exploring practice, it is important to realize that it is often more difficult to get at than first appears. There is often a gap between what people (including you) say and believe that they do and what they actually do. Thus, self-report may not capture the data you need. Other methods are mediated by the values of the person undertaking the analysis.

Each of us has values that we espouse. Many teachers can articulate them in relation to certain criteria. For example, most of us believe in equal opportunity. You may want to dig deeper than this to explore how equal opportunities are defined by students and teachers and how these definitions are or may be incompatible. The series explores the values that are held by each of the stakeholders in education, the implications of these for teaching, learning and management, and the extent to which they are compatible or raise dilemmas that must be resolved. For example, in Chapter 4 we explore the dilemmas raised by investigating the experiences of the least powerful groups of students, point to the dangers of regarding them as people who have things done to them and for them by 'experts', and the need for you, as a researcher, to involve the students in the research design, rather than to treat them as 'subjects'.

Perspectives to be Researched

Reflective practice is about taking account of the viewpoints of others and the long- as well as the short-term consequences of your action. For this reason, the series covers the investigation of a variety of perspectives, particularly different student groups.

Each of these groups has its own priorities and the people within them have their own needs and frustrations. The quality of the services that an institution provides in support of student learning is in part determined by its response to these perspectives.

Research Issues Covered in the Books

A range of research issues are suggested within each book in the series. One of the most important of these is intimately related to values and practice: the perceptions of each of the stakeholders on various aspects of the educative process. Perceptions are closely related to attitudes, in that attitudes are the filter through which we see and judge reality. Attitudes are central to motivation and so to learning. This book will enable you to start to explore the attitudes of students and lecturers to aspects of educational experience.

The link between attitudes and behaviour may be more or less direct. Actual behaviour is influenced by beliefs, but does not always seem compatible with those beliefs. Reflective practice explores the gap and the link between beliefs, implicit theories of teaching and learning and actual behaviour.

Attitudes, perceptions and behaviour are part of the cocktail that influences educational priorities. The educational and non-educational priorities of each of the stakeholders in education are interesting in themselves, and also in the extent to which they are compatible. Understanding competing priorities can sometimes transform a seeming dilemma and enable new ways forward to be found. Moral choice becomes more possible when these are understood.

Typically, at a time of limited resources, prioritization focuses upon the different value given to efficiency and effectiveness. Efficiency and

11

effectiveness are highly topical concerns in colleges and universities. Each may be measured in different ways and each will affect all aspects of the students' learning experience.

Underlying almost every controversy in education are differences in definitions of the problems education faces and the criteria by which success or failure in dealing with these problems may be judged. Because these definitions intimately affect any judgements made, objectivity in educational research may be a false goal. The strength of insider research is that it can recognize and explore ambiguity. The investigations within this book may help you to explore and articulate the values that underpin criteria and definitions used in judgement. For instance, we look at concepts of reliability and validity, and invite you to consider how the political climate influences how these are defined.

The educative process can be viewed in terms of its objectives, processes or outcomes. Each of these implies a different view of what education is about. Each is worth exploring in its own right and from the point of view of the various parties. The most interesting investigation may be into the compatibility of each with the others in real classroom conditions.

Education is a complex interactive human process. For this reason it depends in a fundamental way on relationships between people. Each party to and group concerned with education is affected by the others. The complexity of this interaction and the effects that it has upon teaching and learning are therefore central concerns of the book.

If you believe that reflective practice requires the teacher to take a moral stance, some positions, such as a racist standpoint, are incompatible with reflective practice. Justice, equality and the ways that student diversity is catered for within education therefore become important areas of investigation. This investigation of the morality of the educative process and institutional function can take many forms. In order to take issues of justice and fairness seriously, you have to consider conflicting interests within education.

Ethics and control issues in learning draw a number of issues together. The exploration of dilemmas, how they are construed by the various parties, the way that good practice might be defined, the way that interests compete and are resolved, raise ethical issues, often closely related to the exercise of power and control. Each of the books in the series explores issues of ethics and control across all of the subject matter that they explore. It is this concern, and the willingness to face the difficult problems that result from it, that characterizes reflective practice.

The Quantitative and Qualitative Research Traditions in Education

Research in education may fall into the quantitative tradition and focus on the collection (usually of large numbers) of numerical data, or into the qualitative tradition and look in depth at a smaller number of instances. It may be focused on 'discovery' or on the improvement of practice.

There is much ideological baggage that now surrounds the qualitative and quantitative traditions in education. You need to get to grips with this debate in order that you understand the strengths and weaknesses of each. Within education there has been a shift from respect for models of research based on the scientific tradition of experimental and quasi-experimental research methods, towards qualitative, descriptive methods within naturalistic settings, first pioneered in subjects such as anthropology and now termed 'ethnographic' methods. Each of these models has its strength and weakness. The qualitative tradition is criticized because of its limited scope, particularity and 'subjectivity', the quantitative tradition because of the triviality of its findings, their lack of application to the real life 'messiness' of classrooms and because most practitioners of such research were expert in research and not in education, and therefore 'spoke' to other researchers, rather than to teachers.

Quantitative research must be judged in its own terms. For instance, questions of usefulness or applicability may not be to the point. Quantitative research is 'good' research if the results are valid and reliable. Reliability (the extent to which the context and results can be replicated) is sometimes over-emphasized at the expense of other aspects of validity, such as the assumptions underpinning the questions asked and categories used.

Research in the qualitative tradition must also be judged by appropriate criteria. It should not be criticized for 'subjectivity', unless it claims to be objective. Such research is often problem-centred and pragmatic, and so the notion of proof becomes irrelevant. The validity of the research depends on the extent to which the situation, actions, causes and effects are described convincingly. The quality of the research may depend on interjudgemental reliability (do the readers, researchers and the actors in the research situation describe and interpret the findings in the same way?) 'Subjective' factors are taken into account in judging its quality: at a pragmatic level (was the problem solved to the satisfaction of all the parties involved?); and at a moral level

(the moral basis of actions by the researcher is often open to scrutiny – did they ask the right question, were they 'up front' about their thoughts, feelings and motives, were the values that underpinned the research made explicit?)

Quantitative research methods in education make claims to reliability because of some kind of objectivity or because the 'test' used has been found to work similarly in other situations (for instance, by other researchers, against other tests, and so on). External validity (the extent to which the results of a study can be generalized to other times and places) is generally a matter of the situation and population studied: the size of sample, its 'typicality' and the categories used. Campbell and Stanley (1963) give one of the best outlines of factors that commonly jeopardize the validity of such research. The researcher may present him or herself as a detached outsider observing a situation or seeking to disprove a hypothesis. Thus, some attempt may be made to control the variables in the situation and many instances of a particular result may be described before it can be considered 'significant'. Statistical significance is determined by a standard statistical test.

The kind of insider research that may be most appropriate to reflective practice occasionally uses experimental methods and 'soft' quantitative techniques, but relies more heavily on the qualitative research tradition. It makes few claims for reliability and external validity. Instead, it seeks to describe a particular situation in all is complexity. For this reason, the control of variables is usually inappropriate. The reader determines whether the results are, or are not, relevant. In order that the reader can answer the question, 'Might this research have some significance to me in my particular situation?', they must know the author's claims to expert knowledge, the extent to which his or her conclusions and interpretation of the situation have been tested against the interpretations of other parties, the assumptions that the researcher made, and his or her emotional responses to issues and those of others. Elliott (1991) provides a good account of the strengths and weaknesses of research within the qualitative research tradition.

Each of the traditions makes its own assumptions about cause and effect. The quantitative tradition presupposes that the truth can be separated from the perspective of the observer. The qualitative tradition implies that truth is intimately connected to the thoughts, feelings and assumptions of the participants in education. One model 'tidies' and simplifies reality in order to look at and analyse it; in the other, the full complexity of (a limited) reality is explored. One might caricature the weaknesses of each by saying that the quantitative tradition says something true in the experimental context, that may be untrue, trivial or unimportant in the reality of the classroom, and the qualitative tradition may say something interesting or important about one situation, but there is no way of knowing whether it is the truth. The quantitative tradition tends to be inductive and the qualitative tradition, deductive. Perhaps the best research studies will use some aspects of each. What is important is that, whatever methods you use, you take the time to find out about the construction of appropriate research instruments and admit to the threats to the validity and reliability of the findings inherent within the approach you take.

Data Collection Techniques

The authors provide you with starting points only for research. There is a very wide range of research methods and approaches open to you. These are described in some detail within the books in the series as follows:

Ashcroft, K, Bigger, S and D Coates, D (1996) *Researching into Equal Opportunities in Colleges and Universities*
Semantic differential tests
Focus group techniques
Attitude tests
Database interrogation
Questionnaires: structured, unstructured and open
Scenario analysis.

Bennett, C, Higgins, C and Foreman-Peck, L (1996) *Researching into Teaching Methods in Colleges and Universities.*
Using IT for qualitative data analysis
Emerging data categories
Action research process
Defining a database
Observation: structured and structured.

Jones, M, Siraj-Blatchford, J and Ashcroft, K (1997) *Researching into Student Learning and Support in Colleges and Universities*
Emerging data categories
Symbolic interactionism
Deconstructionism.

Ashcroft, K and Palacio, D (1996) *Researching into Evaluation and Assessment in Colleges and Universities*
Action research process
Validity and reliability.

Higgins, C, Reading, J and Taylor, P (1996) *Researching into Learning Resources in Colleges and Universities*
Systems analysis.

Below we introduce the major strengths and weaknesses of each main research method, and refer you to other sources where you can read more about the technical issues involved in using the research tools you have chosen – see the annotated reading list at the end of this chapter.

Most of the research suggested in the series is small-scale and local and so we do not discuss methods of statistical analysis. It may be that you become inspired to undertake a more major study, in which case there are a variety of computer programs that may help you to analyse your data (see Bennett *et al.*,1996), or you may find a book such as Cohen and Manion (1985) useful. If you intend to use statistical analysis, it is important that you make this decision at the start of the data collection process. The method you use will affect the form of the data you should collect. You will probably find all sorts of problems if you collect your data and then look round for a means of analysing it.

Questionnaires provide a means of obtaining information about people's attitudes, thoughts and feelings in a relatively time-efficient way. They cannot tell you much about actual behaviour since what people say and what they do are not always the same. Questionnaires may be more or less structured. The advantage of structured questionnaires is that, in closing the response options that you allow, you make it possible to handle more data and to compare one set of data with another. On the other hand, unstructured or semi-structured questionnaires allow the respondents to express more exactly what they wish to say. In this sense they are a more accurate reflection of reality. Unfortunately, the very richness of the data makes them difficult to handle. It requires you to impose some sort of order, so that you can communicate trends and issues to your audience. This may oversimplify the responses in the same way as a more structured questionnaire.

The data that questionnaires yield are only as good as the returns you get and questions you use. You will usually get a better return if you can hand the questionnaires to a group to fill in in your presence. The construction of a questionnaire is a skilled matter. For instance, you will need to ensure that your questions are not ambiguous, that they get at what you think they do and that they are expressed simply and in a non-threatening way.

Standardized tests are commonly in the form of questionnaires. They are useful for getting at issues such as learning or management style and attitudes and beliefs. Like questionnaires or interviews, they are not good at describing behaviour. For example, so-called aptitude tests do not describe what you will actually do in a given situation, but merely predict how well you will perform according to the similarity of your responses to those of people doing that job, or your ability as gauged by fairly crude measures in areas such as problem-solving, literacy and numeracy. Standardized tests have the advantage that they have been validated professionally and so enable you to compare your findings with those obtained in other times and places, but you may need to clear copyright to use them.

Interviews share the problems and advantages of the questionnaire, except that they are much more time-consuming to carry out, but yield richer data. There may be more of a tendency for the respondents to say what they think you wish to hear. This may be a particular problem in insider research, where the respondents may have a personal relationship with you and where issues of power (yours over them, or theirs over you) may intrude and make truly honest responses difficult.

One form of interview that enables you to get open responses from a number of people without the problem of obtaining data that are too unmanageable is the group interview. In the form of focus groups, this technique has been used effectively within market research and is beginning to be applied in education (Davies and Headington, 1995). The group interview enables a number of respondents to express themselves in their own way and for you to check out with the respondents your interpretation of what they are saying and the ways you might categorize their responses. You thereby avoid some of the problems of other unstructured techniques. However, some respondents may influence the others' responses unduly and some may be disempowered or find it hard to express themselves in a group situation. Group interviewing is thus a skilled business.

Observation is probably the only way of getting at behaviour, but it may not tell you about motivation, thoughts, feelings and attitudes. Observation may be unstructured: for example, fly-on-the-wall descriptions of what is happening in a situation. A structured observation schedule may enable you to count the frequency of particular pieces of behaviour. If you use structured observation, you are likely to find your data fairly easy to handle, but you may find that categorizing behaviour is not at all straightforward in practice. If this is not recognized in the way you present your findings, you may make your conclusions appear more clear cut than they are. On the other hand, you will probably have to impose order on your fly-on-the-wall observations. Again, you will probably have to simplify reality in order to do so.

Scenario analysis is one way of eliciting people's deeper thoughts and feelings. Scenarios can be presented to respondents in the form of pictures, stories or using some other medium. You might then ask them to explore various aspects of their response. You could record these responses using any one of a variety of structured and unstructured instruments.

Scenarios tend to be contrived to enable you to get at whatever issue you are interested in. Another form of data collection that requires less direct intervention, and so is perhaps less disturbing to the data, is biographical writing (see, for instance, Connolly and Clandinin, 1990; Cortazzi, 1993). In biographical or narrative analysis, you ask respondents to describe significant events, with some guidance from you as to the aspects that they should focus upon. For example, if you were interested in the factors that enable women to succeed with their studies, you might ask several successful women to produce a 'story', not necessarily in words: you can use other techniques such as asking respondents to depict their life as a journey, road or a 'temperature' chart, showing the peaks and troughs in their lives, related to particular events. The data can then be analysed for particular patterns of influence. As with all forms of stimulated recall, you need to be aware that what people tell you, and what they believe about their history, especially their more significant or more remote history, may be clouded by a number of factors. While biography can tell you about people's perceptions, it does not necessarily tell you about what actually happened nor what was cause and what was effect.

Diaries and field notes allow you to collect a range of information as it occurs, using question and answer techniques with individuals or groups, observations and so on, in order to analyse and interpret it at a later date (see for instance, Burgess, 1984, for suggestions as to how to go about this). You can also ask others to keep diaries for you in order to capture their experience more immediately. This technique allows you to explore phenomena in as natural a setting as possible. On the other hand, it does rely on you (or your subjects) noticing and recording significant events, generally in the course of a busy day. This can be difficult.

From the discussion of data collection methods above, it is clear that structured techniques require you to determine categories of response before you start. In order to do so with any confidence, you may have to undertake a pilot study of some kind or to test your hunches about categories in some way. More unstructured techniques require you to explore the data once they are collected to find what categories emerge.

There is a wealth of interesting evidence to be gleaned from systems analysis and the interrogation of databases within your institution. They will contain data that relate to student admissions, locations, subjects and their progress; library and other purchases and stock; personnel; various sorts of accounts; institutional statistics that relate to the physical and learning environment; and performance indicators that may be used for a variety of purposes. Alternatively, you might explore the way that systems are experienced by one or other of the parties to education or the way people and items are categorized.

Documents are part of the public face of institutional activity. Examining the hidden messages within them can be useful and interesting. Documents affect relationships within the institution at all levels. They influence operations and strategy within the institution and are of interest if you want to explore the match between the aspirations of the various parties to education and institutional policies. It can be interesting to analyse what people say, what they do and the way that they present themselves. For example, you might look at the ways that members of certain groups are reflected in official documents, or the ways that expressed aims are or are not reflected in other documents.

You might wish to create other records that can be explored in some depth. For example, you might video, tape-record or photograph certain situations in order to analyse what was going on.

Case studies provide a means of bringing a range of techniques to bear in order to describe what is going on in a particular situation or with a particular group of people. As such, they are especially useful with the kind of insider research that is trying to get at a complex issue. They enable the researcher to use a variety of data collection techniques to look at a variety of viewpoints. Somebody, generally the person who has collected them, has to interpret the data. For this reason, a case study cannot be 'objective' nor does it automatically ascribe cause and effect without bias. Interpretations should, where possible, be checked with respondents to maximize the validity of the findings.

The important thing is never to claim more for your research than is justified by your methods, the data you have collected and your analysis. Insider research can sometimes empower the reader, who may be inspired by a report of research into practice that chimes with their own experience. It is almost impossible to prove anything in education.

Main Issues and Topics Covered in this Book

This book looks at the support students need for their learning, from a relatively wide perspective. It is not primarily concerned with those aspects that are generally dealt with by 'Student Services', although counselling and financial support are mentioned. Rather, it is concerned with the issues and research potential within the support that institutions and lecturers give to the student, the ways that barriers to learning may be increased or minimized, and the extent to which the student is recognized as a valid stakeholder in institutional processes.

In Chapter 2 we consider the context for student support and some of the issues involved. We take the reader through the process of carrying out a literature review. We then go on to discuss notions of validity in enquiry contexts, and relate these to various value positions (for instance, those that may be held by quantitative and qualitative researchers). Student involvement in educational decision making and evaluation are discussed as problematic issues. Action research is explored as a method of looking at improving student experience.

Chapter 3 considers the role of the tutor in helping the student with their personal development and with personal problems. We distinguish between counselling and educational tutoring. The rest of the chapter is focused on the problems that students face in moving into a college or university environment. These problems may be the result of relocation and accommodation, and are looked at in the context of the power relationships that may be involved. The effects of students' financial difficulties are discussed in some depth. Students' choice of course and the availability of advice and Access Funds are considered before an exploration of issues facing returning students. Finally, issues related to student progression are examined.

Chapter 4 looks at the representation and participation of students from various groups. We explore the notion of students as consumers of education, with rights and expectations, in the context of an analysis of equality of opportunity. The needs and voice of disabled students are examined, including the location and definition of the 'problem' of special educational needs. We discuss some of the effects on students of institutional and individual racism, together with the needs of black and ethnic minority students for support in certain contexts. We introduce issues affecting the educational experiences and choices of female and male students before we consider a few of the issues raised by the socio-economic structure of colleges and universities. We look at the problems faced by homosexual, lesbian and bisexual students and their particular support needs. Finally, we consider student representation on institutional committees and the extent to which they are able to make an impact on policy and practice.

Chapter 5 looks at teaching and learning processes, especially within the curriculum context. We explore various approaches to the analysis of the curriculum. The processes of discourse analysis and deconstruction are described as ways of taking into account issues of power. Symbolic interactionism is introduced as one way of understanding the interaction between individuals and groups and their environment. Finally, we consider the role of reflection in linking theory and practice and illustrate this with a detailed case study.

In Chapter 6, we look at issues of power in colleges and universities and the ways that these impact on the lecturer/student relationship. We begin by analysing the notion of micro-politics within an institution. We then go on to discuss effective teaching in terms of student empowerment. A case study of excellence in teaching and learning is outlined in some detail. Critical pedagogy is explored from the standpoint of equality of opportunity and we introduce the role of affinity groupings and/or collective experience in supporting students' learning. Finally, we examine value positions that enable students to engage in critical reflection and students and lecturers to challenge established teaching and research practices.

Chapter 7 is the series conclusion. In it I discuss ways of getting published, the process of writing and the importance of developing a sense of audience. I include an annotated list of journals that publish educational research in the area of student support. I also include an annotated list of book publishers, the kinds of books they are interested in publishing and the lists they are currently developing.

Annotated Reading List

Argyris, C and Schon, D (1974) *Theory into Practice,*Beckenham: Croom Helm.
    The definitive book on the relationships between the theories that people
    hold about their teaching and the theories that they develop in action.
Ashworth, A and Harvey, R (1993) *Quality in Further and Higher Education,*
    London: Jessica Kingsley.
    An account of Total Quality Management, performance indicators, and
    systems for assessing standards.
Bell, J (1987) *Doing your Research Project,* Buckingham: Open University Press.
    This book deals with research across the disciplines, rather than teaching
    and learning in further and higher education.

Brown, S, Jones, G and Rawnsley, S (eds) (1993) *Observing Teaching,* Birmingham: *Staff and Educational Development Association.*
This focuses on inquiring into practice in colleges and universities. It covers issues in the appraisal of teaching (who should do it, what should be observed and how). The focus is on professional development, rather than research within higher education.

Cohen, L and Manion, L (1985) *Research Methods in Education* (2nd edn), Beckenham: Croom Helm.
A comprehensive account of the major research methods in education. It is not easy to read, and I would argue with its assumption that educational research should be 'scientific', but its critique of the approach we adopt provides a useful counterbalance. The book covers most of the techniques in educational research, as well as more technical aspects such as Grid analysis and multidimensional measurement.

Gibbs, G *et al. 53 Interesting Things to do...,*Bristol: TES.
This series is very popular and sells well (one book is in its fourth edition since 1986). The books are about 140 to 160 pages long and provide some useful starting points for thinking about teaching and learning. The focus is on practice, rather than research, but this can provide you with a starting point for an evaluation or intervention study.

Green, D (1993) *What is Quality in Higher Education?* Buckingham: Open University Press.
A report of a national research project on the assessment of quality in higher education.

Hammersley, M and Atkinson, P (1983) *Ethnography Principles in Practice,* London: Tavistock.
A reasonably accessible account of ethnographic methods and their relationship to the social world. It includes a critical analysis of case study, observation, interviewing and ways of filing and recording data.

McKernan, J (1991) *Curriculum Action Research: A handbook of methods and resources for the reflective practitioner,* London: Kogan Page.
This book is a good introduction to action research. It contains many useful suggestions for collecting data.

Smith, B and Brown, S (eds) (1994) *Research, Teaching and Learning in Higher Education,* London: Kogan Page.
A collection of reports of research undertaken by experienced education developers within higher education.

References

Argyris, C and Schon, D (1974) *Theory into Practice,* Beckenham: Croom Helm.
Ashcroft, K (1987) 'The history of an innovation', *Assessment and Evaluation in Higher Education,* 12, 1, 37–45.
Ashcroft, K Bigger, S and Coates, D (1996) *Researching into Equal Opportunities in Colleges and Universities,* London: Kogan Page.

Ashcroft, K and Foreman-Peck, L (1995) *The Lecturer's Guide to Quality and Standards in Colleges and Universities*, London: Falmer Press.

Ashcroft, K and Griffiths M (1989) 'Reflective teachers and reflective tutors: School experience in and initial teacher education course', *Journal of Education for Teaching*, 15, 1, 35–52 .

Ashcroft, K and Griffiths, M (1990) 'Action research in initial teacher education', in Zuber-Skerritt, O (ed.) *Action Research in Higher Education*, Brisbane: Griffith University Press.

Ashcroft, K and Palacio, D (1996) *Researching into Assessment and Evaluation in Colleges and Universities*, London: Kogan Page

Ashcroft, K and Peacock, E (1993) 'An evaluation of the progress, experience and employability of mature students on the BEd course at Westminster College, Oxford', *Assessment and Evaluation in Higher Education*, 18, 1, 57–70.

Ashcroft, K and Tann, S (1988) 'Beyond building a better checklist: development in a school experience programme', *Journal of Assessment and Evaluation in Higher Education*, 14, 1, 61–72.

Bennett, C, Foreman-Peck, F and Higgins, C (1996) *Researching into Teaching Methods in Colleges and Universities*, London: Kogan Page.

Burgess, R (1984) 'Keeping a research diary', in Bell, J and Goulding, S (eds) *Conducting Small Scale Investigations in Education Management*, London: Harper and Row.

Campbell, D T and Stanley, J C (1963) *Experimental and Quasi-Experimental Designs for Research*, Chicago, Ill: Rand McNally.

Carr, W and Kemmis, S (1986) *Becoming Critical: Knowing through action research*, London: Falmer Press.

Cohen, L and Manion, L (1985) *Research Methods in Education* (2nd edn), Beckenham: Croom Helm.

Connolly, F M and Clandinin, D J (1990) 'Stories of experience and narrative enquiry', *Educational Researcher*, 19, 5, 2–14.

Cortazzi, M (1993) *Narrative Analysis*, London: Falmer Press.

Davies, S and Headington, R (1995) 'The focus group as an educational research method', *British Educational Research Association Annual Conference*, Oxford: October.

Deakin University (1982) *The Action Research Reader*, Victoria: Deakin University Press.

Dewey, J (1916) *Democracy and Education*, New York: The Free Press.

Elliott, J (1991) *Action Research for Educational Change*, Buckingham: Open University Press.

Higgins, C , Reading, J and Taylor, P (1996) *Researching into Learning Resources in Colleges and Universities*, London: Kogan Page.

Higher Education Funding Council for England (1994) *1996 Research Assessment Exercise*, June, Bristol: HEFCE.

Irwin, A (1995) 'Gypsy professors roam US campuses', *The Times Higher Education Supplement*, 24 February.

Isaac, J and Ashcroft, K (1986) 'A leap into the practical', in Nias, J and Groundwater-Smith, S (eds) *The Enquiring Teacher: Supporting and sustaining teacher research*, London: Falmer Press.

Stenhouse, L (1979) 'What is action research?', *CARE*, University of East Anglia, Norwich, mimeograph.

Zeichner, K (1982) 'Reflective teaching and field-based experience in teacher education', *Interchange*, 12, 4, 1–2.

Zeichner, K and Teitlebaum, K (1982) 'Personalised and inquiry oriented education: An analysis of two approaches to the development of curriculum in field-based experience', *Journal of Education for Teaching*, 8, 2, 95–117.

Chapter 2

Education or Training in Colleges and Universities?

The Context for Student Support

The support that students may expect from colleges and universities is determined by a number of factors. Among these is the notion of the student as a 'consumer' of education, although, unlike other consumers, students do not usually pay for the full cost of their education. The idea of the student as consumer stems in part from the pressures on institutions to meet recruitment targets in order to avoid losing resources, but in addition, in the UK, consumerism has been encouraged by the government, and codified in the *National Charter for Further Education* (DfE, 1993a) and the *Charter for Higher Education* (DfE, 1993b). These documents require institutions to involve students in institutional decision-making and set standards (or in the case of higher education, encourage institutions to set standards) for processes such as the quality and timing of information and response to applications and complaints in relation to courses, qualifications, facilities, fees, entry requirements and student services. You might like to investigate the ways that institutions in each of the further and higher education sectors have been influenced by these Charters and the opportunities and threats they pose to such institutions, compared to the benefits they bring to students.

RESEARCH TASK. INVESTIGATING STUDENT CONCERNS

Talk to a group of students in a college or a university.

Discuss with them the extent to which the Charters reflect students' real concerns about student support service in colleges and universities.

Read about one of the concerns that seems to be an issue for a number of students.

You may find these topics and related publications useful starting points:

Resources for learning – Follett Report (1993)
Support for student-centred learning – CNAA (1992)
Support for work-based learning – HEQC (1994)
Personal support for students – Civil (1991)
Vocational preparation – FEU (1982)
Support for special educational needs – FEFC (1994).

Kleeman (1991) gives a useful general introduction to students' concerns.
Record your reading in an annotated reading list (see research task below).

Issues in Student Support

Students may need to be supported in a variety of ways. Some have considerable experience and qualifications and may be able to achieve a university or other qualification in less time than others, and may need to be introduced to systems for the accreditation of prior learning. They may need help in presenting their experience in appropriate ways, so that it can be fully taken into account.

Many students find that university or college education brings with it considerable changes. Many of these changes and the stresses that come with them are discussed elsewhere in this book in some detail. The process of education can sometimes transform students' sense of 'self'. This may bring crises in marriage, religious faith or other difficulties that may require the services of a chaplaincy or access to spiritual or secular guidance. You might wish to explore the extent to which such guidance is made available to students of different faiths, in various sectors of the education system.

Some students may get into difficulties or trouble that they will not be able to sort out easily for themselves. Caring institutions are likely to have systems of self-advocacy to ensure that students' voices are heard, and that they are empowered to articulate their 'case': for instance, for help, leniency or grievance.

So that lecturers can provide students with the help that they need, and in order that they can protect themselves from accusations that they have failed to provide appropriate help, it is important that adequate records are kept of pastoral and other non-teaching interactions with students, including discussions about progress and personal problems. You might wish to investigate what records various practitioners and experts in the fields of teaching and student support feel should be kept, what records practitioners actually keep, and to what uses such records are put.

Aims and Objectives of Colleges and Universities

The support system of an institution should be reflected in its aims and objectives. These will often be found embodied in its mission and policy statements. Whether they are drawn from formal institutional statements or the implicit assumptions of HEQC guidelines, broad perspectives and definitions often provide a valuable background for questions. It is often possible to identify the perspectives of the various stakeholders in the education process: for instance, the academic community, employers, students and funders. These may be employed to provide a grounding for subsequent research and analysis. As Adelman and Alexander (1982) have suggested:

> policy formulation and institutional decision-making ought to be subject to an approach analogous to scientific inquiry, namely, one of constant critical examination using the experience of implementing policy not as a means of proving, whatever the cost, that the policy was right but as a means of testing its validity, strengths and weaknesses. (p.171)

The further education curriculum is often assumed to be of a broadly vocational nature. Frankel and Reeves (1996) describe a more complex reality. They see it as representing a heterogeneous federation of curricula that draws upon a variety of different educational traditions. Higher education has also been founded upon many of the same and, perhaps, some additional scholarly traditions. In both sectors many of the stakeholders see the educational provision as having important possibilities for cultural change and for social regeneration (Ainley, 1994). One of the key questions in education today concerns the relative emphasis placed upon education and vocational 'training': should our courses focus on the acquisition of transferable skills and understandings or should they be determined by narrowly focused competences?

You could consider how *your* institution defines its aims and how these are related to the stated policies on issues such as student guidance and learner support. The arrangements within your institution may be consistent or diverse. There may be tensions within the system that manifest themselves in different ways. Your investigations might reveal differences between the aims of the institution and the staff and student perceptions regarding their realization. Any one or all of these issues offer possible starting points for a research study concerned with developing practice in the area of student learning and support.

In many studies, these concerns will be discussed in an introductory review of the literature and it is to this subject we now turn. We continue our discussion of institutional aims in Chapter 5, where we identify some principles of deconstruction.

Review and Analysis of the Literature

There are those who favour an extreme version of 'emergent theory', where existing models and theories are seen as limiting possible interpretations of data. This may be a real problem, but we have found that the inexperienced researcher may be able to work more productively if she or he takes account of the collected wisdom, gleaned in other times and places. This knowledge is usually gained through a study of the literature. However, readers should be aware of the Internet as an increasingly useful source of recent research and data (although they should also be aware that most is subject to no quality control).

Ideally, a literature review constitutes a continuous process that extends throughout your study. In your final presentation, the literature review should, as far as possible, locate your study within the most relevant theoretical and/or research traditions that have preceded it. It is also important to recognize the significance of your review to the analysis of what you find in the field, especially that part of the analysis concerned with data reduction. The amount of data that might be collected about virtually any educational process or phenomena is very great. Some choice and selection is necessary if data are to be manageable. Miles and Huberman (1994) have provided a useful flow model that illustrates the various components of data analysis; this is shown in Figure 2.1.

As you first select the particular subject and analytical framework for your study, you will reject some of the many possible sources and forms of data that you might collect. Your initial reading, life experiences and values contribute towards this anticipatory data reduction; they also contribute towards an ongoing reduction. It is important that you carry out some degree of introspection in order to become aware of your reasons for favouring particular research questions, conceptual frameworks and data collection techniques.

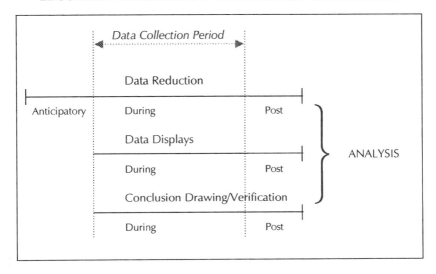

Figure 2.1 *Data collection and analysis (from Miles and Huberman, 1994)*

'Data displays' in Figure 2.1 refer to the organization, compression and assembly of information. This will be discussed further in Chapter 6, when we will also suggest an outline structure for a research report. In the meantime something more needs to be said about the process of conclusion drawing and verification. From the earliest stages, the researcher decides what things mean. As a researcher, you will note regularities and patterns, and will start to formulate explanations and possibilities. The trick is to hold these very lightly to begin with: to be sceptical. As you move forward, you may refer back to your earlier notes, and check with respondents and documentary evidence. You may even attempt to replicate your initial findings. These strategies are employed to test your findings for plausibility, to confirm your assumptions and to demonstrate their validity.

It is important to recognize that your review of the literature will, itself, provide the initial basis for your readers' evaluation of the validity of your study. If the research is to be prepared for publication, the introductory review will establish your credibility as a researcher. It may need to convey enough of the background and importance of your 'problem area' to introduce a non-specialist (and perhaps uncommitted) reader to your field of interest. All of the work that you do on the review at these early stages is likely to help you to sharpen-up and limit your research question to an area that will support in-depth study.

RESEARCH TASK. ANNOTATED BIBLIOGRAPHY

At the beginning and throughout the research process, the compilation of a well organized annotated bibliography can provide a very useful source of reference to inform your analysis. It can also save you hours in the library as you prepare the paper for publication.

Prepare an annotated bibliography by keeping records of all your reading as follows:

- Make sure that you include the full bibliographic details. In addition to the authors/editors and publication date, in the case of chapters, research papers and journal articles, note the relevant page numbers and, where appropriate, volume and issue number. For books, note the publisher and the place of publication.
- Include just enough information to identify the text, the general theme covered and the particular value/relevance of it for your study, for example:

  Siraj-Blatchford, J (1996) Teaching Technology, Science and Social Justice, London: Education Now Books (ISBN 1 871526 25 6)
  This book provides practical advice for primary and lower secondary teachers of science and design technology. It takes a global anti-racism perspective and includes a number of illustrations of curriculum approaches to developing children's awareness of multicultural values in science and design technology. The illustrations include an extended consideration of structures, of vernacular buildings, and of electronic technologies. It is argued that in these later cases a systems approach might often be useful and electronic circuits and devices may be treated as 'black boxes'.

In your reading and in the writing of your annotated bibliography remember to:

- look out for a conceptual framework which can form the basis for the organization and structure of your study;
- assess the quality of the work you review so that the best sources are given more weight (ask yourself when, where, by whom and how the studies were conducted);
- attempt to arrive at general conclusions about the current research related to your topic;
- identify areas where authors suggest that future research is needed, especially where they may set the stage for your study in the introduction to your research;
- clarify definitions, assumptions and limitations that underpin the material you read.

Evaluation, Values and Validity

Most case study research involves some form of evaluation. This is a process of identifying the values within the research and in the situation. This tends to be true whether the case study is concerned with illuminative and summative evaluations or with the kind of experimental and formative evaluations typical of action research (see Bennett *et al.*, 1996, and Ashcroft and Palacio, 1996, for more on the process and principles of action research).

Cronbach (1982) has argued that the design of evaluative investigation is something of an art. Evaluations may be summative or formative. They may be bureaucratic; for example, the product of contract research. They may be autocratic; for example, where they are produced by an expert adviser. Alternatively, they may be more democratically framed (see, for example, MacDonald,1987). Another possibility is where an *illuminative* perspective is employed; in this case the:

> attempted measurement of 'educational products' is abandoned for intensive study of the programme as a whole: its rationale and evaluation, its operations, achievements, and difficulties. The innovation is not examined in isolation, but in the school [or college] context or 'learning milieu'. (Parlett and Hamilton, 1987)

Illuminative approaches typically emphasize the mediated nature of the instructional system and see learning as occurring within a complex cultural environment.

Evaluations may be presented subjectively or objectively (see Burrell and Morgan, 1979). Your selection will be determined by your choice of epistemology (epistemology refers to your 'way of knowing' – very often framed in terms of a particular discipline). It will also be influenced by your perceptions of the general nature of knowledge claims.

Many researchers are, quite understandably, concerned about the reliability and validity of their research, These concerns are often closely associated with the ideas about what constitutes science and scientific knowledge. Broadly, a firmly objective approach will be taken by those who favour positivist 'hard scientific' epistemological approaches. In these cases, a quantitative statistical methodology is likely to be employed. Those who wish to make more modest claims for their results are more likely to adopt qualitative methodological techniques.

As Iram Siraj-Blatchford (1994) argues, to most quantitative researchers, validity is about 'truth conditions': the relationship between what it is that a test measures and what it will predict (Guildford, 1954).

By contrast, qualitative case study researchers are often more interested in what seems to be true than in the truth *per se.* They attempt to portray the world as it appears to the people that are inhabiting it.

It is significant that the words 'valid' and 'value' have the same etymological roots. For an idea to have value or to be valid is for it to be strong and effective. Our assessments of validity are based upon our perceptions of 'worth' and hence upon our value systems. In clarifying our rationale we delegate to our reader some degree of the responsibility for assessing validity. The reader may then accept or reject our explicit values. As Siraj-Blatchford (1994) says: 'Quantitative researchers... often present their findings as objective truth and hence smuggle their values in' (p.18).

Burrell and Morgan (1979) usefully discriminate between those researchers who favour discourses associated with the politics of regulation and those who favour the promotion of radical change. Inevitably, your contribution will itself be evaluated according to your audience's perceptions of your own position on these dimensions.

There are many controversies in social science and in education and many of the disagreements cross disciplinary boundaries. There are sociological and psychological theories of learning and within individual disciplines there are alternative theoretical frameworks. Educationists would like to know whether group or individual study is more effective; whether the size of groups is significant; whether mixed ability teaching is more effective than setting and streaming, whether single subject teaching is superior to more integrated approaches. While we may, as individuals, prefer certainty, our decisions are often based upon balancing the risks of error against the potential benefits of a particular course of action. We may be informed by the available evidence but, ultimately, involved in value judgements. This is not peculiar to social science: mainstream science has its own controversies. Scientists disagree about the evidence for an enhanced greenhouse effect due to the burning of fossil fuels, about the risks associated with BSE entering our food chain; whether hormone replacement therapies endanger women's health in the long term; and whether food irradiation will lead to lower health risks or whether the long-term risks outweigh the short-term benefits.

A good researcher has a healthy scepticism and a willingness to weigh the evidence to arrive at balanced conclusions. It is important to be aware that no matter how much data you collect that 'fit' with your theoretical model or explanation, they will never guarantee it as the 'truth'. Popper (1959) argues that it is only through the falsification of theory that scientific knowledge can move forward. A classic example illustrates this: you may see many white swans and conclude that all swans are white; however, seeing one black swan will conclusively falsify the hypothesis.

Unfortunately, educational matters are less subject to notions of 'truth'. Our choice of hypothesis depends upon the direction that our observations take and these are based upon our value system. If we consider the colour of swans to be significant, we may live with the scientifically corroborated belief that all swans are white for many years. Research studies are always partial accounts and involve the selection of a focus, of relevant evidence and of arguments at every stage. The quantitative/qualitative distinction is rather misleading – we are all both quantitative and qualitative, we all search for recurring data and yet, for the more qualitative researcher, the overall emphasis is not so much on the quantity of data collected but rather on its quality, breadth or depth.

There are two further terms worth considering: reliability and replicability. To the quantitative researcher, reliability is to do with the degree of fit between the data and our theoretical representation of them. On the other hand, in case study work, we attempt to collect multiple representations, to show different definitions and to present our research in a manner that is open to multiple interpretations. In so far as we are successful in this, reliability becomes the concern of our reader rather than of us as researchers.

The associated problem of replicability – whether another researcher would produce the same results – is usually solved by providing a clear and explicit account of our research process. The reader is able to follow the researcher's footsteps, so to speak, and assess the rationale at every stage.

Adelman and Alexander (1982) have argued for integrity in the face of 'the risk of evaluation's use, abuse or neutralisation to further or protect individual or sectional interests...'. They suggest that evaluative integrity should be based on:

● eclecticism (for example, using a variety of techniques);
● triangulation (for example, consulting a range of sources of data);
● acting as the 'underdog's advocate';
● valuing the intuitive judgements of 'ourselves and others';
● a willingness to re-evaluate our evaluation.

RESEARCH TASK. INTERVIEWS: EVALUATION OF AN INSTITUTIONAL ISSUE

Identify the aims of your institution with regard to some aspect of student support.

Track how these have been put into practice within the institution. Identify:

- the systems that are in place;
- what is intended in terms of future development.

Use your analysis as a framework within which to explore the perspectives of managers, staff and students with regard to a particular issue: for instance study facilities or personal support issues.

Conduct a semi-structured interview with a few managers about their perspectives on the issue. From your results, identify an agenda which includes:

- key aims in relation to the issues;
- the management perspective on their implementation.

At the same time, clarify and follow up on key issues as they emerge.

Use this as the framework for constructing a structured questionnaire that will allow you to explore the perspectives of staff and students on those aims and areas concerned with the implementation of policy.

Discuss your questions, your expectations of what they would reveal and what particular responses might signify with a small group of staff and students. Refine your questionnaire in the light of their feedback.

(See Billing, 1986, or Duke, 1992, Ch.3, for more on this kind of evaluation.)

Student Involvement, Morale and Academic Self-image

One area of potential research is student involvement. Students get involved in many ways in the life of a college or university. They may sit on various committees; they run many clubs and societies; have involvement in the National Union of Students; they are asked to provide feedback on courses; and get involved in new staff appointments. This involvement varies from institution to institution. It may be an important factor in student morale and relate to encouragement and to academic self-image.

In many institutions, students are involved in course evaluation on a regular basis. If neither staff nor students are to be dissatisfied by the process, this may need to be handled in a sensitive way. It may not be possible for a student to identify with the aspirations that a lecturer has for them. Even when the objectives for the course are clear to the students, they may have their own agenda. Evaluative feedback responses may be concerned with the students' perceptions influenced by their own personal agendas rather than the lecturers'. If students are required to provide useful judgements about the content of teaching programmes and modules, they may need the kind of overview which allows them to do so.

In many subject areas, there are clearly defined approaches that determine not only the content of the course but also the teaching strategies that are used. In many cases, students' short-term needs may not match the tutors' long-term concerns. In teacher education for example, students are often concerned to build up a repertoire of lesson blueprints that they can apply successfully in the classroom. Yet few lessons can be guaranteed to work with all children and so a course structured in this way might be impractical. The tutor recognizes that students need to learn general principles that they will apply as professionals in generating their own lessons. The teacher educator may decide that it is inappropriate to respond to student evaluations that suggest a greater emphasis on the presentation of 'good lessons plans'.

The situation described above provides an example of the tension between narrow vocational interests and more open-ended educational interests in higher education at the level of the seminar room or lecture theatre. Themes such as these may run through an evaluative study and the philosophical arguments applied to inform the analysis of data collected at a variety of levels.

RESEARCH TASK. COURSE EVALUATION

Evaluation of courses can provide useful data for informing institutional direction and curriculum development. Run an evaluation session with students towards the end of a course, as follows:

- set up a group brainstorm;
- ask the students to identify aspects of the course they think should be included in an evaluation sheet;
- contribute your own objectives of the course;
- put the products of the brainstorm and the objectives that have been agreed on display;
- ask the students individually to write on any aspects they choose.

Typically this process will yield at least one side of A4 paper from each participant. The problem then becomes one of analysis. The data are not easy to analyse because the information is not clearly structured. Yet this may also be considered an advantage as the terms of the students evaluation have not been prejudged either. The trick is to pull out the common themes or 'reduce the data' through analysis and this is a skill (or art) in itself. Carry out the process as follows:

- identify different issues in each student's writing;
- cut the paper so that each 'issue' is separated;
- classify the resulting issues into 'types';
- sort the students' responses into these categories.

If the task is to be carried out manually a good deal of space may be required. The main alternative is to use a computer, and a variety of appropriate software packages are available. Programs such as Ethnography, NUDIST, Qualpro and Text Analysis can be very useful in speeding up this stage of the research process.

Alternative course evaluation methods to that outlined above involve providing a much more structured list of questions. The following format, used in a course in teaching primary mathematics, provides an example.

Objectives for the course:
To increase personal confidence with and understanding of mathematics.
To increase awareness of 'how children learn'.
To consider teaching approaches and resources for all areas of the National Curriculum.
To consider some of the issues in mathematics education, eg, the use of calculators.
To consider the role of the coordinator and issues relating to it.

Questions:
1. To what extent do you think the objectives of the course have been addressed?
2. Which elements of the course have you (a) enjoyed? (b) found useful?
3. Which elements of the course have been of little personal use to you?
4. Do you have any suggestions for next year?
5. If you could change one thing what would it be?

In this example, the course objectives are included up front and the questions are designed to encourage constructive criticism to take place.

The student responses may acknowledge that the course included elements that they personally did not need, but indicate a recognition that other group members did. Valuable suggestions may be made that could be applied to the course planning for the following year.

Of course, these examples are not the only ways of collecting feedback. Some suggestions for further reading, which include other methods, can be found at the end of the chapter or in Ashcroft and Palacio (1996). Evaluations may be rushed at the end of the course and this in itself can lead to tutors obtaining some disappointing feedback.

You might, for instance, survey the practices of other colleagues to find out the format their evaluation sheets take and other ways of obtaining the information desired. University of Leeds (1992) includes a section on consulting students through questionnaires which points to the strengths and shortcomings of using evaluative questionnaires and discusses issues you may need to consider when designing your own. Ashcroft *et al.* (1996) describes in some detail one method of creating a questionnaire.

Action Research

Student feedback may also identify problems with the course that you wish to remedy through research. Such studies may be based on the sort of classroom-based action research inspired by Stenhouse's (1975) conception of the 'extended professional' seeking 'autonomous self-development'. As Elliot (1991, pp.49–50) has noted:

> The fundamental aim of action research is to improve practice rather than to produce knowledge. The production and utilisation of knowledge is subordinate to this aim. The improvement of practice consists of realising those values which constitute its ends, eg 'justice' for legal practice, 'patient care' for medicine, 'preserving the peace' for policing, 'education' for teaching....The reflective practitioner's understanding of the values (s)he attempts to realise in practice are continually transformed in the process of reflecting about such attempts. Values constitute ever-receding standards.

Kemmis (1983) has provided a useful model of the processes of action research.

The example provided in Figure 2.2 relates to a project carried out by a school teacher researching her own classroom practice. Applied more generally to research in colleges and universities, we would be concerned that the model was used less instrumentally. The teacher in the example makes a number of assumptions that a more sophisticated researcher would problematize. A more thorough study would question further what is was that constituted the most appropriate science curriculum for the students involved. It would draw upon the reports of other research projects and upon theory in order to justify its initial plans. As stated earlier, much of this work would be covered in some form of introductory literature review.

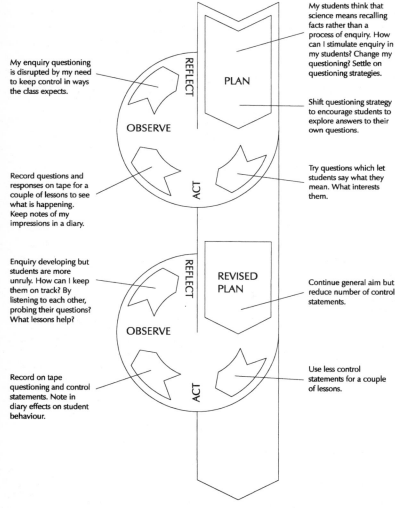

Figure 2.2 *The process of action research (from Hopkins, 1985)*

A thorough action research study would also self-consciously address itself to the problem of validation. Hopkins (1985) suggests two techniques that may be employed to achieve validity in this kind of study: 'saturation' and 'triangulation'.

Saturation (Glaser and Strauss, 1967) refers to the process whereby each of the researchers' ongoing interpretations of events (their hypothesis or intuitions) is repeatedly tested against the data in an attempt to falsify it. Through testing, it may be rejected, modified or elaborated. This is an application of Popper's (1959) falsification principle – from this perspective our understanding may never be considered entirely complete but at some point it may be considered fairly reliable. This model draws on a 'scientific' notion of validity and may be criticized if you take the view that the value of research is in the extent to which it yields data that can be recognized as 'true' or 'valuable' by people in a given situation.

Triangulation is a validation process first popularized by Elliott and Adelman (1976) that answers some of these problems. In this case, authenticity is demonstrated by showing a relatively small difference between the perceptions of one actor against another in the same situation. For example, a teaching situation might be viewed from three different points of view: that of the teacher/tutor, the students and a participant observer. Another approach to validation through triangulation is to use more than one data collection technique: for example, the validation of observational data through interview. Yet another strategy is to involve a colleague in the process of interpretation. A very effective strategy that has been employed by action research groups of school teachers and nurses has been to meet regularly and to share and discuss their various projects among themselves. Such groups constitute a 'critical community' where rules of confidentiality have been agreed, the various forms of planning and methods are discussed, and researchers are able to provide each other with practical support in their 'progressive refocusing'.

RESEARCH TASK. ACTION RESEARCH: EVALUATION FORMATS

Undertake an action research project into the format of your own or your institution's evaluation according to the following process.

Identify a problem with your evaluation (for example, whether the present format of evaluation sheets is as useful as it might be for curriculum development).

Use the action research model to enquire into the context of the problem, to decide on a possible intervention and to investigate the effectiveness of that intervention. At each stage:

- share your planning and reflection with one or more colleagues; and
- keep detailed notes about what you did, your conversations with colleagues, what happened, and your reflections, as they occur.

The process of action research involves undertaking at least two cycles of enquiry as follows (adapted from Kemmis, 1983):

- Identify the problem that will be the focus for your enquiry:
  Whose problem is it (yours, the students', course managers');
  Why is it important (because you are not getting the information you need, because students do not feel able to get their point of view across)?

- Find out as much as you can about the context in which it occurs:
  What is happening now?
  Why is it a problem?
  What form does it take?
  What are the alternative explanations for the problem?
  (For instance, you might ask what information you currently take from students; what are your purposes in collecting this information; does it inform future planning or a report to the management team; is the method fit for the purpose intended?)

- Discuss your interpretation of the problem with colleagues and/or students.
  Decide on an intervention that might improve the situation:
  What might a better situation look like?
  Why would it be better?

- Plan the intervention in some detail:
  What actions might improve the situation?
  How should they be sequenced?
  What criteria would indicate 'success' in dealing with the situation?
  (For instance, try developing several different formats for an evaluation sheet, and decide which formats are likely to give you the information you need for the purposes you have identified.)

- Discuss your plan with colleagues and/or students.

- Implement the plan (for instance, trial various formats of evaluation sheets with different groups).

- Collect data on the effectiveness of your plan:
  What techniques did you use to collect your data?
  What were the advantages and disadvantages of each?

How might you triangulate findings (can you seek views from various participants in the process, or use more than one data collection technique)?

- Evaluate the data:
  Do any key words or phases recur in your written records?
  Do your data need re-examining in more detail?
  Are your data sufficient to draw conclusions or inferences?

- Discuss your evaluation with colleagues and/or students.

- Review and if necessary revise the plan:
  Are new ways of looking at the problem emerging from the data?
  Does your initial focus or research question need to be reformulated?
  What values and assumptions about evaluation were implied by your original approach?
  Do these need revising?
  What ethical issues are raised by your research?

- Discuss your plan with colleagues and/or students.

- Implement the revised plan.

- Repeat the data collection/evaluation cycle.

Write up your research for one of the journals that specialize in action research in education.

Annotated Reading List

Burgess, R (1993) *Research Methods,* Walton-on-Thames: Nelson.
  A comprehensive look at research methods currently in use.
Cohen, L and Manion, L (1994) *Research Methods in Education,* London: Routledge.
  Covers the whole range of research methods employed by researchers. This is the latest in a series of regular updates of this publication.
Ramsden, P and Dodds, A (1989) *Improving Teaching and Courses: A guide to evaluation,* Melbourne: University of Melbourne.
  Outlines a range of evaluation strategies for teaching and for courses.
Rose, G (1982) *Deciphering Sociological Research,* Basingstoke: Macmillan.
  Key issues of methodology are demonstrated within the framework of a systematic deciphering of research.

References

Adelman, C and Alexander, R J (1982) *The Self-evaluating Institution – Practices and principles in the management of educational change,* London: Methuen.

Ainley, P (1994) *Degrees of Difference: Higher education in the 1990s,* London: Lawrence and Wishart.

Ashcroft, K and Palacio, D (1996) *Researching into Assessment and Evaluation in Colleges and Universities,* London: Kogan Page.

Ashcroft, K, Bigger, S and Coates, D (1996) *Researching into Equal Opportunities in Colleges and Universities,* London: Kogan Page.

Bennett, C, Higgins, C and Foreman-Peck, L (1996) *Researching into Teaching Methods in Colleges and Universities,* London: Kogan Page.

Billing, D (1986) 'Judging institutions', in Moodie, G C (ed.) *Standards and Criteria in Higher Education,* London: SRHE and NFER-Nelson.

Burrell, G and Morgan, G (1979) *Sociological Paradigms and Organisational Analysis,* Aldershot: Gower.

Civil, J (1991) 'Managing student services', *Coombe Lodge Report,* 22, 8, 639–87.

CNAA (1992) *Case Studies in Student Centred Learning: CNAA Project Report 36,* London: Council for National Academic Awards.

Cronbach, L (1982) *Designing Evaluations of Educational and Social Programs,* San Francisco, CA: Jossey-Bass.

DfE (1993a) *Further Choice and Quality: National Charter for Further Education,* London: Department for Education.

DfE (1993b) *Higher Choice and Quality: The Charter for Higher Education,* London: Department for Education.

Duke, C (1992) *The Learning University. Towards a new paradigm?,* Buckingham: Open University Press.

Elliot, J (1991) *Action Research for Educational Change,* Buckingham: Open University Press.

Elliott, J and Adelman, C (1976) 'Innovation at the classroom level: a case study of the Ford teaching project for the OU Course E203', *Curriculum Design and Development,* Milton Keynes: Open University.

FEFC (1994) *Disability, Learning Difficulties and Further Education,* Coventry: Further Education Funding Council.

FEU (1982) *Tutoring: The guidance and counselling role of the tutor in vocational preparation,* London: NICEC and Further Education Unit.

Follett, B (1993) *Joint Funding Council's Libraries Review Group Report,* Bristol: HEFCE, SHEFC, HEFCW and DENI.

Frankel, A and Reeves, F (1996) *The Further Education Curriculum in England – An introduction,* Wolverhampton: Bilston College Publications.

Gibbs, G, Habeshaw, S and Habeshaw, T (1983) *53 Interesting Ways to Appraise your Teaching,* Bristol: Technical and Educational Services.

Glaser, B and Strauss, A (1967) *The Discovery of Grounded Theory,* Chicago, Ill: Aldine.

Guildford, J (1954) *Psychometric Methods,* New York: MacGraw Hill.

HEQC (1994) *Higher Education Projects, Digest 1, Summer,* London: Higher Education Quality Council.

Hopkins, D (1985) *A Teacher's Guide to Classroom Research,* Buckingham: Open University Press.

Kemmis, S (1983) 'Action research', in Husen, T and Postlethwaite, T (eds) *International Encyclopaedia of Education: Research and Studies,* Kidlington: Pergamon.

Kleeman, A (1991) 'Student issues and concerns', *Coombe Lodge Report,* 22, 8, 695–702.

MacDonald, B (1987) 'Evaluation and control of education', in Tawney, D (ed.) *Curriculum Evaluation Today: Trends and implications,* Basingstoke: Macmillan.

Miles, M and Huberman, A (1994) *A Qualitative Data Analysis (2nd edn),* London: Sage.

Parlett, M and Hamilton, D (1987) 'Evaluation as illumination', in Murphy, R and Torrance, H (eds) *Evaluating Education: Issues and methods,* London: Harper and Row.

Popper, K (1959) *The Logic of Scientific Discovery,* London: Hutchinson.

Siraj-Blatchford, I (1994) *Praxis makes Perfect: Critical educational research for social justice,* Nottingham, Education Now.

Stenhouse, L (1975) *Introduction to Curriculum Research and Development,* Oxford: Heinemann.

University of Leeds (1992) *Evaluating Teaching and Learning: Collecting and using feedback from students and other sources,* Leeds: University of Leeds.

Chapter 3
Student Perspectives and Problems

Students tend to learn more effectively when good support systems are there to help them cope with the transition between the academic world and their previous experiences. The transition is difficult for a number of reasons and, for many, may include the move from a sheltered parental home to an independent life. The difficulties may be different for mature students, some of whom may have given up financial security to pursue a route involving years of financial insecurity without the guarantee of a job at the conclusion of their studies.

All sections of the student body may be affected by a variety of other problems that may impact on their ability to make the most of their study opportunities. In this chapter, we raise some of the issues related to effective study. Since very little research in this area exists, carrying out your research into aspects of student perspectives and problems could prove to be both interesting and original. The issues are discussed within a UK context, but many of the research opportunities outlined in this chapter can be adapted to apply to the non-UK reader, who is asked to read and generalize the problems within their own institutional and cultural contexts.

A good starting point for you to begin considering support services might be to look at the work carried out by the Further Education Unit (1993). This research identifies the range of learner support services and the proportion of colleges that have a particular service. For instance, 79 per cent of further education colleges have a counselling service on site. The research looks at supporting the learner as well as the learning. It also considers the quality of learner support services in this sector of post-16 education.

The UK HEQC *Guidelines* (1995) state that institutions are responsible for 'supporting and cooperating with student-led organizations and services providing support, information and practical advice services to learners'. The intention is for you to consider a number of issues which might lead to an evaluation into the effectiveness of your institution's provision of support. Students who are not beset by a range of problems are more able to take advantage of the course of study offered to them. The need to deal with problems saps energy which otherwise could be channelled into study.

In this chapter we examine some of the principles that underpin educational tutoring and counselling, before exploring the problems that may face new and returning students. There are several problems that may be faced by first-year students; you may wish to investigate which are most common and which experiences emerge in combinations. These problems may emerge under the following three categories that are examined separately: relocation and accommodation, financial, and poor choice of course.

Counselling and Educational Tutoring

It is important to be clear about what constitutes educational tutoring (and therefore the responsibility of every lecturer) and counselling (a much more specialized activity, that on occasions may involve skills and commitments with which the individual lecturer is not equipped to cope). Educational tutoring generally takes the form of a regular programme of events directed at supporting students' academic development: for instance, their ability to set themselves educational objectives and monitor their own progress towards them, their ability to recognize their strengths and weakness, or the development of study skills.

Educational tutoring is very often concerned with the monitoring of student progress. Where such progress is giving cause for concern, educational tutoring may be supplemented by educational counselling. This enables the tutor to facilitate the student's exploration of the ways that the hidden and overt curriculum are, or are not supporting their learning. Together the tutor and the student may look at the student's expectations and behaviour: for instance, to investigate the ways that unconscious or conscious messages about study, educational authority, values and expectations may be causing the student problems, or causing the student to create their own problems.

Educational counselling is therefore problem-centred and may be related to an academic crisis or to remediating a long-standing problem with a student's work. It may be focused around help with study problems, misunderstandings, confidence, discrimination and conflict. It may be about the development of knowledge and skills or about helping the student to develop more appropriate attitudes and behaviour. Some areas of educational counselling are much more sensitive and require much more skill and training than others.

The skills of educational tutoring, and to some extent educational counselling, are similar to those used in appraisal of performance in any work setting. You might look at the extent to which the design of the support system and the people operating within it are clear on whether it is primarily about development of students' own 'professionalism' as students, and therefore an empowering process, or whether it is about remediating and eliminating poor performance. If the system is primarily designed for the first purpose, you might wish to investigate how remediation is handled. If the system is sometimes adapted for remediation purposes, you could look at how (or whether) this change of purpose is signalled to the student and the effects on the student when the signals are not clear.

Counselling generally involves working within the affective domain: that is, dealing with the emotional baggage that people accumulate that gets in the way of them functioning as well as they otherwise might.

Counsellors usually work within one of a number of clear frameworks. Some of these, such as those within the behaviourist and psychoanalytic traditions, we believe to be inappropriate outside of a therapeutic context and so we do not discuss them here. One useful framework for analysing the counselling situation is drawn from the humanist psychological tradition, and is perhaps best exemplified by Rogers (1983). He talks about the contexts and attitudes that underpin successful counselling. He suggests that the student can only be helped through the necessary emotional learning in the absence of threat and where learning is seen as relevant to their needs and interests, and is voluntary. He sees the development of certain qualities as important in the educational counsellor. These include having an unconditionally positive regard for the student, a genuineness of approach and empathy (the ability to think yourself into the students' shoes – this is not the same as identification).

Geldard (1989), working within this tradition, identifies basic counselling skills, including:

- listening skills (listening to the words, but also what is behind them);
- non-verbal skills, including the ability to mirror the student's behaviour;
- taking time to reflect before responding (this implies a tolerance of silence);
- paraphrasing what the student says – to check and reflect back meanings;
- questioning – especially asking few, but open questions;
- summarizing;

- confrontation (although this needs great care);
- terminating an interview.

You may wish to use particular 'languages' developed within the humanistic tradition to analyse what is going on in counselling situations. Although the ideas have been around for some time, that of transactional analysis (Berne, 1964 or Harris, 1970) or of assertiveness training (Dickson, 1982) are still useful. If the situations that you wish to look at are concerned with the development of learning styles or study skills, you could start with the work of Entwistle (1981) or Kolb (1984)

In investigating counselling situations and analysing what is occurring within them, the researcher will need to be aware of many ethical issues. These will include issues of confidentiality, as well as the harm that a researcher can do either by intruding on a situation where there is likely to be a delicate balance of power between the student and the tutor, or by reporting and describing what is going on in ways that may not reflect the students' perspective and, on occasions, may be damaging to their view of themselves.

Educational counselling has some skills and processes in common with therapeutic counselling, but most lecturers are not equipped to handle therapeutic situations. You could look at where the lines are drawn in various contexts between what is a legitimate lecturer concern and where such concern should stop. It is important that tutors recognize their own limitations and when and where to look for help in this respect. It is our contention that, as a general rule, tutors should not engage in therapeutic counselling. This is because, although there are some similarities in role, there are important differences between what a lecturer and a counsellor can offer a student.

RESEARCH TASK. INVESTIGATING THE COUNSELLING ROLE

Read Geldard (1989) to find out more about counselling and the skills and processes it involves.

List what you believe are the differences between educational and therapeutic counselling; for example, in educational counselling:

- the goals of the counselling may be set (at least in part) by the lecturer;
- the time that may be given to the counselling may be limited;
- the lecturer will not be in a position to be totally non-judgmental (for instance, about racist attitudes and behaviour);
- the lecturer will not be able to promise confidentiality;
- the problem may be identified by the lecturer rather than the student;

- the 'help' may not be totally voluntary (for instance, the student may fear that they will fail the course if they do not take the advice offered);
- the lecturer is in a different power relationship to the student than a therapeutic counsellor.

Interview a number of tutors within one or more institutions to find out what problems they would and would not help their students to tackle. Try and establish the 'boundaries' to their help (for instance, in terms of the time they would devote).

Write a paper on the extent to which lecturers may stray into areas of therapeutic counselling, and the dangers that may be inherent in this. Draw conclusions in the form of recommended dos and dont's of educational counselling.

One interesting area for investigation is that of students' personal and interpersonal skills development throughout a course. You could look at what skills students feel that they have developed and the extent to which this perception is shared by lecturers. You could also look at the extent to which lecturers feel that it is important to develop such skills in their students and, where they feel that it is an important objective, how they recognize, define and assess them.

Some lecturers believe that it is the role of the teacher to help students to become aware of their assumptions and values and how these affect their learning and behaviour. It seems likely that such awareness of the interpersonal context for action extends the options open to students. You might investigate the ways in which lecturers include such skill development in the curriculum (overt and hidden) and what teaching methods they employ.

We now move from a discussion of students' problems and personal development in general terms to look at some specific issues and problems that many of them face and their implications for the support that students are offered.

Relocation and Accommodation

The first problem a student may have to deal with once they have been accepted into a higher education establishment is that of residential accommodation.

You might investigate students' experience of and feelings about finding somewhere to live in an area often unknown to the student or student's parents. There may be a limited choice in many university cities or towns of suitable, affordable accommodation. In addition, many students find themselves in a communal environment with limited control over their choice of companions. Students may have to deal with property-owners who are less than scrupulous. A fruitful area of investigation is the support a 'fresher' may expect from their institution and the extent to which this varies from college to college, university to university, from student union to student union and even from year to year in each of these structures.

Higher education establishments may provide some accommodation in halls of residence. Some promise all first-year students a place in halls. In the UK, this is more commonly found in the old universities. The level of service within halls may vary greatly, from full board and porter service at a premium rent to basic self-catering accommodation at below private sector rents. You might investigate the preferences of different groups of students. Blakey (1994) looks particularly at universities and colleges as suppliers of student accommodation within the institution and how this affects recruitment and choice of course, as well as considering briefly the private sector, which accounts for 65 per cent of student accommodation.

You might look at the extent to which the residential accommodation available influences students' decision to come to your college or university. Other studies which will provide useful background in this field of research are Alstead (1991) and Carver and Martin (1989).

The case of unscrupulous property-owners is a particularly interesting one. You may wish to consider the issues raised when the property-owner is the university or college that is also in control of that student's qualification. An imbalance of power may occur for those students in halls of residence or property-managed houses (that is, accommodation in the private sector administered on behalf of the property-owner, by the institution). You may wish to investigate the extent to which the students are required to give up their autonomy from the institution in order to receive a more reliable assurance of quality accommodation, and what happens when the student is dissatisfied with the service being provided. For instance, in the private sector, it is not unusual for individual members of a house to withhold rent from their property-owner, or deduct an appropriate amount. It is clearly much harder for dissatisfied tenants of the institution to withhold rent from their institution. If they do so, they may risk being prevented from re-registering for their course, or being asked to leave altogether. In many cases the full rent and board is deducted at the start of each term, making it impossible to withhold this money.

You could investigate the outcomes where the student union acts as intermediary and the effectiveness of systems such as hall committees. You could look at the extent to which problems can be communicated to the institution by the hall student representative, or if problems tend to be beyond their skills, or occur outside of the halls, or how often an independent arbitrator, such as the welfare officer, may become involved.

Where the student is at fault in the eyes of the institution, you may wish to investigate the grounds for disciplinary procedures against the student. You could also explore the experience of students once disciplinary procedures are initiated: for instance, whether they are informed of their right to representation through the student union, or their view of the effectiveness of such representation.

Many universities will provide accommodation lists in which property-owners advertise their properties. These provide the student with a ready-made list of addresses, usually divided into the different areas. While this system does provide a useful service, it may be impracticable for an institution to run detailed checks on all properties and property-owners. It is possible that a number of students will end up in accommodation with which they will become dissatisfied. You may wish to investigate the extent of dissatisfaction, the reasons for this and whether there is a pattern.

You could look in detail at the various contractual and legal aspects of student life, and the awareness of students who are relocating for their courses as to what constitutes a good deal and what is a bad one; what is a fair contract and what is not; what a property-owner is reasonably entitled to ask of them and vice-versa; the latest health and safety regulations regarding rented accommodation; or a host of other issues related to their tenancies.

The final issue here is the problem of ill-matched house- or room-mates. You could investigate whether this can be dealt with effectively if the student is moving to an area without any of their previous friends. Some institutions try to deal with this problem by using questionnaires to match students suitably, prior to their arrival on campus. If your institution uses this method you may wish to explore its success (or otherwise) and what students and institutional managers think of the system. In some institutions many management and study hours are lost dealing with the traumas arising from ill-matched couples, especially where they have to share a room.

The problems of close living have led some colleges and universities to come up with student guidelines for sharing accommodation on campus. Below is a set of guidelines issued to students at one college.

'Surviving on Site': 10 Commandments

1. Do nothing which causes difficulty, harm, irritation, or which intrudes into the life of any other member of the community.
2. Make no noise
   - after 11pm from Sunday to Thursday
   - after 1am on Friday and Saturday.
3. Do what you do quietly.
4. Do not abuse fire alarms.
5. Do not entertain guests without the agreement of your room mate.
6. Respect your cleaner and make sure she (sic) has access to your room.
7. Have no pets.
8. Use no drugs.
9. Respect the grounds
   - do not walk on the grass
   - do pick up litter.
10. Do not walk across the by-pass.

Observance of these rules will lead to a happy life.

FAILURE TO OBSERVE THESE RULES MIGHT RESULT IN DEATH
OR EXPULSION FROM RESIDENCE.

On the surface some guidelines (including some elements of those above) may seem strange to the reader and some background might help to put them into context. You might wish to explore rules and guidelines from a range of institutions, their origins and effects. For instance, in the case of the college above, there have been problems with all-night visitors to shared rooms and hence the reason for 'commandment' number five. The grass at the college is on a very thin layer of top-soil and is easily destroyed, hence number nine. There has been a death caused by a student crossing the by-pass, hence number ten and also the reference to death in the sentence in capitals at the end. You could look whether relatively trivial rules being listed alongside more important ones appear to affect the students' attitudes to these rules and their behaviour. Boyer (1990) provides information on students' attitudes towards moral issues on campus; he shows that 56 per cent of all students interviewed thought that the colleges should provide a code of conduct for students. His report on campus life for the Carnegie Foundation provides a background to many of the issues associated with life on campus as well as a wealth of research statistics in this field.

You might also look at the level of detail within institutional rules and guidelines, the forms they take and whether they have guidance which arises from the particular circumstances at the campus. You might analyse the categories into which the rules and guidance fall (for instance, rules that deal with moral issues, health and safety issues, social issues or administrative convenience) and who is the principal beneficiary of each category of rules or guidance (for instance, the student, other students or the property-owner).

You may wish to consider how student grievances are dealt with in your institution with respect to its owned or managed accommodation. You could investigate the difference between the types of problems faced by students in external accommodation and those in halls of residence. You will need to be aware that this may be a sensitive area for both your institution and the students, particularly with regard to the power issues raised. Collecting data may not be easy. You may not be seen by the students as a sympathetic or disinterested party, with no axe of your own to grind. Your research may be destined to be published within a public forum and students may be wary of communicating information that they feel is not completely anonymous. For areas of particular sensitivity, it may be that a questionnaire, in which the respondent remains anonymous, is the only way forward. This may not solve all you problems: for instance, your institution may not wish negative findings to be published. Your own concerns over student recruitment in a competitive climate may tempt you to give your data a favourable 'spin'.

RESEARCH TASK. QUESTIONNAIRE SURVEY: STUDENTS' EXPERIENCE IN RELATION TO ACCOMMODATION

Undertake a survey to find out the range and severity of the problems faced by first-year students in relation to accommodation. Decide upon some subsidiary issues which you will wish to explore. These issues might include:

- how suitable accommodation is found;
- charges made to students for accommodation;
- personal problems adjusting to communal life;
- property-owners and tenancy agreements.

Define your objectives clearly before you begin; for instance:

- To collect information on the types of accommodation occupied by the current first-year students in my institution.
- To investigate whether students were assisted by the institution in finding the accommodation.

- How many students live:
  in halls;
  in private residences;
  at home;
  in some other form of accommodation?

- How many was the accommodation found:
  independently;
  by the institution;
  in some other way?

- How satisfied are the students in each category with:
  their accommodation;
  the way it was found?

- In what ways do they think that the system could be improved for:
  approving accommodation;
  finding accommodation;
  monitoring accommodation.

- What features of accommodation do they feel to be particularly important?

In constructing the questionnaire there are a number of issues which you might wish to consider. Questionnaires are useful for obtaining information about people's:

- attitudes;
- thoughts; and
- feelings.

They are not so good for getting at:

- actual behaviour; and
- complex situations.

The advantages of structured questionnaires are that:

- you can handle more data; and
- you can compare one set of data with another.

The disadvantages of structured questionnaires are that they:

- close the range of the responses that you allow;
- force you to predict, and so predetermine, categories of response.

The advantages of unstructured or semi-structured questionnaires are that they:

- allow the respondents to express more exactly what they wish to say;
- allow a more 'accurate' reflection of reality.

The disadvantages of unstructured or semi-structured questionnaires are that:

- the richness of the data makes them difficult to handle;
- you must impose some sort of order, so that you can communicate trends and issues to your audience;
- you may oversimplify the responses;
- you may misinterpret the responses.

The data that questionnaires yield are only as good as the questions you use and the returns you get. You will usually get a better return if you can hand the questionnaires to a group to fill in in your presence.

In order to construct a good questionnaire you should ensure that:

- your questions are not ambiguous;
- they get at what you think they do;
- they are expressed simply and in an unthreatening way.

(See Ashcroft et al., 1996, for details on how to construct a questionnaire.) Data will need to be checked for:

- completeness – all questions have been answered;
- accuracy – no careless mistakes have been made by interviewee or respondent; and
- uniformity – instructions have been interpreted uniformly.

Then the data will need to be coded so that they can be processed. For example, if we take the issue of the finding of suitable accommodation, a tick-box questionnaire could have the following form:

How did you find your current accommodation? (Please tick one or more of the following, as applicable):

College/university found accommodation in halls ☐
College/university found accommodation in a private residence ☐
I found the accommodation myself through:
  (i) an agency ☐
  (ii) a newspaper advertisement ☐
  (iii) other ☐ Please specify: _____
I still reside at home with my parents ☐
Other ☐

Since a tick is required in a single box it is easy to set up a simple count code for each of the students who completes.

A more informative open-ended approach, but one that is less easy to analyse, might be to ask:

Could you describe how you came to find accommodation on entering college or university?

This could be coded by identifying specific features, which could be followed up at a later stage, but might lead to information being offered which could be difficult to code.

Roberts and Higgins (1992) carried out research looking at student life and collected data on types of accommodation and the ease with which students found that accommodation. Contrast your findings for your particular institution with their findings. Ask yourself:

- How is the position different?
- If you are working in a UK institution and there are differences, is this because there have been changes or because you feel your institution is fundamentally different from the national picture?
- If you are working in a non-UK institution, how is the picture different?
- How can these variations be explained in terms of the local circumstances that prevail?

A useful source of national data which will allow you to make local comparisons are the UK Annual Accommodation Surveys commissioned by the National Union of Students.

Financial Problems

In the UK, the first financial problem many students in higher education will face is finding the deposit to secure accommodation. Students can expect to pay one month's rent as deposit as well as one month's rent in advance. This may be a considerable outlay before the student has even moved in or picked up their first grant cheque.

Banks will often have branches set up on the main campus, and may have specific knowledge of student issues. Setting up a bank account or gaining access to a grant may be made more difficult by the process of registering for the course itself. In the UK, if a student has come through clearing (the system which places late applicants and those not placed earlier), they may not be able to register for their course at the same time as other students. It may take some time for their registration form to be processed. Without this form it is not possible for a student to pick up their grant cheques, apply for assistance from Access Funds or register their student status with the Community Charge Office. If a student has applied late for a grant to their Local Education Authority, their grant cheque may not be waiting for them at the institution and the payment of fees for the course may also be delayed, in which case the student may not be able to register for their course.

In the UK, the student union can become involved on behalf of the student. Students may need a bit of encouragement from the union in certain situations, sometimes just giving them the information they need to deal with the problem themselves. (See the UK research of Augusterson and Foley, 1989, who were commissioned by the National Union of Students to carry out a survey into students' financial positions.) An effective welfare officer or welfare department will often establish a relationship with the campus bank and university admissions department, which may have a degree of flexibility in dealing with these situations. Welfare services within the institution itself may also give advice on these issues. You could look at non-UK institutions which deal with these types of problems and whether the welfare services are run by the institutions or the students themselves.

The National Union of Students published a report (Gaines, 1985) on student loans. The research in the report focuses on four countries: Denmark, Sweden, the United States and Canada, and considers the student loan system in those countries. It contains information on the views of governments, students and banks. It considers issues such as access, gender, race and social class, as well as levels of debt and parental loans. It is a good source of information for anyone wishing to research the area of student financial problems because it anticipated many of the issues that have emerged as the loan system has been implemented in the UK.

RESEARCH TASK. INTERVIEWS: STUDENTS' FINANCIAL PROBLEMS

Interview a cross-section of students to discover their personal financial situation. In forming questions for students in individual interviews, some of the issues might be:

- Are they entitled to a grant?
- Is the grant mandatory or discretionary?
- If they are entitled to a grant, was the grant waiting on their arrival at your institution?
- What gap is there between their arrival at the institution and the collection of any grant?
- How was that gap bridged (for instance, loan from parents, bank, access fund)?
- Do they need to supplement the grant?
- Do they work for the institution or another employer?
- What effect do they believe this is having on their study habits and time?

In conducting the interviews, bear in mind that interviews share the problems and advantages of the questionnaire (outlined in the previous research task). In addition:

- they are much more time-consuming to deliver;
- there may be more of a tendency for the respondents to say what they think you wish to hear;
- they may be inappropriate where the respondents have a personal relationship with you and where issues of power (yours over them, or theirs over you), *but* –
- they can yield richer data.

One of the issues in UK institutions is the fact that institutions themselves employ students, often on a very poor wage, to carry out tasks such as kitchen or cleaning duties. You might look at the perspectives of those involved in this practice. The college management and the students themselves may have a positive view of this in that both might feel they benefit from the system. Others may take the view that such employment could prevent the institution from certifying to Local Educational Authorities that the student is studying full-time. You might explore the views of the wider community, who may consider this to be exploitation, particularly if students' ability to study is undermined by their employment, or tutors, who may worry about the effects on students' study.

Students who are in courses in further education may have a different set of financial problems. Often students, particularly those who are part-time, have no grant, although some may be funded by employers for their course of study. Many have to pay fees and all expenses while still holding down a job. Many of them also have families to support. In general, a higher percentage tend to come from the lower socio-economic groups. The research task outlined previously will need to be adapted if you are carrying out your research in an institution of further education or its equivalent in non-UK countries.

Poor Choice of Course

Generally, after about four or five weeks, most first-year students have a fairly good idea of whether or not they are happy at the institution they have chosen. It usually takes a little longer to decide whether or not the course itself is living up to their expectations. Should the student decide that the institution or the course is not what they hoped it would be, it may be possible for them to change their course within the institution, move to another institution, or to leave the course with the option of taking up a place at a later date. These decisions may be subject to places being available on other courses, the student fitting the course criteria and, in the UK, the government's Mandatory Grants and Awards Regulations. The student union will often liaise with faculties and course leaders in order to advise the student on the best course of action to take.

In the UK, institutions face financial penalties when students leave for another institution and may be reluctant to see such a move as in the student's best interest.

Movement between institutions may rely upon liaison between organizations. This can result in students suffering from poor advice: for example, a student may change course on advice and, because of the regulations governing mandatory awards, find themselves without a grant for the following year or required to return part or all of their grant. You could investigate the operation of advice and liaison services in various institutions. Alternatively, you could compare similar problems within different national contexts.

RESEARCH TASK. COMPARATIVE STUDY: INSTITUTIONAL COOPERATION AND COLLABORATION

In conjunction with a colleague at a partner institution in another country, investigate the situations that exist with regard to students' entry and movement between courses. Look closely at the way in which each institution deals with this particular problem.

Review policy statements and/or written material supplied to the students by several colleges or universities. Documents are part of the public face of institutional activity. Examining the hidden messages within them can be useful and interesting. Documents can:

- affect relationships within the institution at all levels;
- influence operations and strategy within the institution;
- be of interest if you want to explore the match between the aspirations of the various parties to education and institutional policies;
- be useful in analysing what people say, what they do and the way that they present themselves;
- be useful in analysing the ways that members of certain groups are reflected in official documents;
- be useful in analysing the ways that expressed aims are or are not reflected in other documents.

Design a questionnaire aimed at students who have changed courses. (See

---

Ashcroft *et al.*, 1996, for detailed guidance on how to construct a question-naire.)

The following questions may be raised:

- Are there factors which mean that students (or particular groups of students) may not be getting the best possible advice?
- If so, what are these factors?
- In what ways are institutions the same?
- What are the differences?

Broadfoot *et al.* (1988) compared French and English attitudes to teaching; in particular focusing on the meaning of professional responsibility. You might use this research to analyse student transfer. You might ask:

- Are there cultural differences which make it easier or harder for students to change course after entry?
- Are there cultural differences with regard to tutors' views of their professional responsibility in this context?
- Are these cultural differences reflected in institutional and course documentation?
- Are these reflected in student responses to your questions?

Problems of Returning Students

There are several different kinds of financial problems for returning students. Pilkington (1994) examined some, including those which have been brought about by a change in circumstances and those which have grown out of a lack of money.

A change in the students' circumstances can take many forms. One of the most common is that of a change in the student's parental income. At the moment in the UK, many students do not qualify for a full maintenance grant because their parents' income is above a certain level. If a change in circumstances occurs, the student can apply for their grant to be reassessed. This may be a relatively straightforward task, but may require time to accumulate all of the necessary paperwork. Meanwhile, the student will be having to operate on a reduced income.

You could explore what happens if the student's circumstances change but they do not qualify for any form of grant or fees payment: for instance, some institutions operate a system of fees remission, under which students who are required to cover the costs of their course fees may have them remitted or waived by the institution.

Windle (1989) carried out a survey of student income and expenditure. This is a good source of facts and figures. It considers both young students and mature students, as well as those on sandwich courses. It looks at income from a number of sources including grants, vacation work and parents. Students' income and expenditure are related back to socio-economic class.

The UK government has set up a pool of money within institutions through the Department for Education and Employment. This money is called the 'Access Fund' and is available for students who find themselves in financial difficulty. It is placed with the institution and the amount is based upon student numbers. This money was put in place as a cushion for students when the entitlement to social benefits over the summer period was removed. However, the criteria for the allocation of this money and their interpretation can vary. As a result, two students in different institutions may be experiencing exactly the same difficulties, but only one will benefit from the Access Fund. It could be interesting to explore the various criteria used to distribute the Fund in various institutions, or the demand for support from students studying on various types of programme.

RESEARCH TASK. DOCUMENT ANALYSIS: INVESTIGATING THE OPERATION OF THE ACCESS FUND

You will need to collect information from a number of institutions about the way in which the Access Fund is administered and the criteria that are used for deciding who should benefit. Collect this information from:

- official documents;
- those who administer the Fund;
- the students union at the institution;
- students who have tried to access the Fund.

Write to several different institutions to collect this information: for instance, you might include in your sample:

- a further education college;
- a college of higher education;
- an old established university;
- a new university;

- other types of institutions which cater for the post-16 age range.

Use the information collected to identify:

- features which are the same or common to all;
- variations which may lead to particular inequalities.

Progression Through Courses

Many courses do not take the first-year results as part of the final qualification grade, but require a pass in end-of-year exams in order for the student to continue on the course. You may wish to look at whether, once a student has progressed through the first year, the pressure to achieve good and consistent grades becomes greater.

With many institutions employing a module-based approach, there is the opportunity for students to highlight their strengths by choosing a particular route through the course. The effect of modularization is itself worthy of investigation. This is a relatively new area and as yet we do not know all of its effects. Some areas that might be worth investigating are the effects on student stress; assessment levels and types of assessment being used; the social problems and opportunities of studying alongside new students in each module; and the lack of linear progression. Some of the problems that may be inherent in modular courses have been identified by Bell and Wade (1993). These include: units of time defining the learning process rather than units of competence; and both attendance and accumulation of marks or credits being identified with worthwhile learning. The other problems are connected to the choices inherent in these types of courses that may threaten the coherence of the learning experience. A fruitful area for research could be how various institutions deal with these problems. Watson (1989) provides a series of interesting articles written by staff at Oxford Polytechnic on this topic.

Whatever difficulties students may face in their course, be it emotional or financial, the solution in terms of seeking help and advice relies on knowledge and communication. For instance, the University of the West of England's Education, Welfare and Information Department produces a range of booklets giving advice to students on academic, welfare and equal opportunities issues, as well as child-care provision. These booklets can be an interesting focus of study in terms of the implicit models of the student and the institutions' response to them.

RESEARCH TASK. INDIVIDUAL AND GROUP INTERVIEWS: INVESTIGATING THE COMMUNICATION SYSTEMS FOR STUDENT HELP

From the discussion of questionnaires in the first research task in this chapter, it is clear that structured techniques require you to determine categories of response before you start. This applies to interviews as well as questionnaires. In order to determine categories with any confidence, you may have to undertake a pilot study of some kind or to test your hunches about them in some way.

More unstructured techniques require you to explore the data once they are collected to find what categories emerge. There are various techniques; see Bennett et al., 1996, for more details.

Carry out a pilot set of fairly unstructured interviews with a small sample of individual students to ascertain their knowledge of procedures. Clarify or broaden the category, by beginning with a number of questions which can be followed up in an informal way. For instance, you might ask them:

- Do you know what to do if you experience financial difficulties?
- Do you know what to do if you experience course difficulties?
- How do you know what to do? Is it by word-of-mouth or can you identify the relevant handbook or pamphlet which outlines procedures?
- Who would you talk to first?
- Do you know if you are going to get impartial advice?

You might focus the rest of the interview on ways they think that the communication systems could be improved. Look at the resulting data to see what categories have emerged that might be explored further.

The group interview has some advantages in common with individual interviews and some particular to itself; for instance, it enables you to get open responses from a number of people without the problem of obtaining data that are too unmanageable. In the form of 'focus groups', this technique has been used effectively within market research and is beginning to be applied in education (see Ashcroft et al., 1996, for more detail on this technique). The group interview enables:

- a number of respondents to express themselves in their own way;
- you to check out with the respondents your interpretation of what they are saying;
- you to check out with the respondents the ways you might categorize their responses.

However:

- some respondents may influence the others' responses unduly;
- some respondents may be disempowered;

> - some respondents may find it hard to express themselves in a group situation.
>
> Follow up your individual interviews with more structured interviews with several groups of students.
>   Explore their experiences of communication systems for student help and their ideas as to how their needs might be better met.

There are a number of issues and factors that will need careful teasing out in order to ascertain how effectively your institution promotes knowledge and its methods of communicating that knowledge with respect to student needs. For instance, if we take the area of financial difficulty, the starting point for investigation might be the students' own definitions of financial difficulty.

When considering the practical problems that students may experience within further and higher education, and which may affect the student's learning you may wish to explore the extent to which you can generalize with a fair degree of confidence.

Most students experience some difficulties during their life in an institution. Problems associated with finance are likely to be ongoing throughout a student's time with an institution. Problems with courses, either because of a poor initial choice or personal, emotional, or stress-related factors, will also arise for many students. The problems with accommodation are likely to be of a seasonal nature.

The research tasks in this chapter will enable you to begin to measure the quality of support your institution gives in this important area and outline some of the real problems which both institutions and students face in more detail, so that developments and improvements can be targeted.

Annotated Reading List

Baldwin, S and Percy-Smith, J (1992) *Financial Hardship Among Students at Leeds Polytechnic,* Leeds: Leeds Metropolitan University.
    Research into student hardship, showing the correlation between student bank overdrafts and the length of course of study.
Buss, R (1993) 'The university viewpoint', in *School of Business and Industrial Management,* Proceedings from a Conference on the Provision of Student Accommodation in the University and National Health Service Sector. Contrasts increases in rents in institutional accommodation with those in the private sector.

Eastham, C (1993) *Accommodation for Students: Case study of the East Moor Project,* Leeds: Unipol Student Homes.
Research into student needs in housing in terms of the standards of housing and the costs of renting.

Further Education Unit (1991) *Flexible Colleges: Access to learning and qualifications in further education, parts 1 and 2,* London: FEU.
Describes features of flexible colleges, spotlighting areas for development. It also considers the issues faced when attempting to widen access, and inhibitors to progress.

Johnes, G (1993) *The Determinants of Student Loan Take-up in the United Kingdom,* Lancaster: Lancaster University.
Research exploring the reasons for the differences in the take-up of student loans between men and women.

London School of Economics (1992) *Report from the Review group on Student Hardship and Services,* London: LSE.
Outlines LSE funds available for student hardship, of which only 11 per cent is from the HEFC hardship Access Fund.

Moon, B (1988) *Modular Curriculum,* London: Paul Chapman.
This book provides an overview of many of the modular curriculum initiatives. It is a series of case studies covering developments in schools, LEAs and TVEI projects.

National Union of Students (1993) *Accommodation Costs Report 92/93,* London: NUS.
How accommodation costs contribute to student hardship. This report also identifies regional differences in charges for accommodation.

National Union of Student Services Ltd (1993) *Student Debt Survey 1993,* London: Barclays Bank
Surveys into the level of student debt.

Oxley, M and Golland, A (1993) 'Student housing: university challenge for the 1990s', *Housing and Town Planning Review,* April/May, 18, 26.
Research which looks at the differences in lengths of students' letting agreements.

Saxby, J (1984) *Undergraduate Income and Expenditure,* London: National Union of Students.
A major survey into hardship, commissioned by the NUS.

Theodossin, E (1986) *The Modular Market,* Bristol: The Further Education Staff College.
An historical look at the development of modular courses in Great Britain. Several case studies of modular courses are included. Links are made between the modular course and the marketing of further and higher education.

References

Alstead, C (1991) *A Report on the Housing Situation for Students at Leeds Polytechnic – with emphasis on the demands for residential accommodation,* Leeds: Leeds Metropolitan University.

Ashcroft, K , Bigger, S and Coates, D (1996) *Researching into Equal Opportunities in Colleges and Universities,* London: Kogan Page.

Augusterson, K and Foley, K (1989) *Opportunity Lost,* London: National Union of Students.

Bell, G H and Wade, W (1993) 'Modular course design', *Journal of Further and Higher Education,* 17, 1, Spring.

Bennett, C, Higgins, C and Foreman-Peck, L (1996) *Researching into Teaching Methods in Colleges and Universities,* London: Kogan Page.

Berne, E (1964) *Games People Play: The psychology of human relationships,* Harmondsworth: Penguin.

Blakey, M (1994) 'Student accommodation', in Haselgrove, S (ed.) *The Student Experience,* Buckingham: Open University Press.

Boyer, E (1990) *Campus Life – in search of community,* Princeton, NJ: Princeton University Press.

Broadfoot, P, Osborn, M with Gilly, M and Paillet, A (1988) 'What professional responsibility means to teachers: national contexts and classroom constants', *British Journal of Social Education,* 9, 3.

Carver, K and Martin, G (1989) *Student Housing and Related Findings,* Rowntree Findings No. 13, York: Joseph Rowntree Memorial Trust.

Dickson, A (1982) *A Woman in Your Own Right,* London: Quartet.

Entwistle, N (1981) *Styles of Learning and Teaching,* Chichester: Wiley.

Further Education Unit (1993) *Learner Support Services in Further Education,* London: FEU.

Gaines, A (1985) *Student Loans: The costs and the consequences,* London: NUS.

Geldard, D (1989) *Basic Professional Counselling: A training manual for counsellors,* New York: Prentice Hall.

Harris, T A (1970) *I'm OK – You're OK,* London: Pan.

Kolb, D A (1984) *Experiential Learning: Experience as the source of learning and development,* Englewood Cliffs, NJ: Prentice Hall.

Pilkington, P (1994) 'Student financial support', in Haselgrove, S (ed.) *The Student Experience,* Buckingham: Open University Press.

Roberts, D and Higgins, T (1992) *Higher Education: The student experience.* Leeds: Heist.

Rogers, C (1983) *Freedom to Learn for the 80s* (2nd edn), Columbus, OH: Charles E Merrill.

UK HEQC (1995) *Guidelines,* London: HEQC.

Watson, D (1989) *Managing the Modular Course. Perspectives from Oxford Polytechnic,* Buckingham: Society for Research into Higher Education and Open University Press.

Windle, R (1989) *Student Income and Expenditure,* London: Research Services Ltd.

Chapter 4

Student Representation, Participation and Action

Colleges and universities in the UK are currently undergoing massive changes. The metaphor of the student as the consumer, 'buying into education' is increasingly used. Often, students are involved in the evaluation, planning and design of their course of study. Student representation may be found in all aspects of college and university life.

Student participation in the committee system of colleges and universities has existed for a very long time, particularly in the UK. The recent trend of extending this participation seems to result in part from right-wing policies, which apply the philosophy of the market place to all aspects of life including education. This has led to considerable debate about the effects of the market philosophy on the quality of education. It appears that, with less financial support from central government, students find it increasingly difficult to support themselves through a sustained course of study and some find they have to work as well. This has implications for the time they have available to devote to private study.

Many of the issues around finance have been considered in the previous chapter. In this chapter, we consider the wider aspects of student life and how students may adjust to the new situation they find themselves in as consumers of education. We explore the ways their expectations, hopes and views of the course in which they are participating may influence its development and delivery.

We also consider the complementary issue of equal opportunities and what we as educators are doing to encourage and implement equal opportunities policies. Clay *et al.* (1995) write that many institutions have 'strong sounding policies' on equal opportunities but few have effective implementation of the policies due to a lack of structure to back them up. We begin by considering the experience of members of various student groupings with respect to equal opportunities. Throughout we explore student representation and self-determination.

Equal Opportunities and Student Representation

As consumers, students also represent a cross-section of society. Institutions that wish to provide a quality education may need to consider the issues that arise from race, gender, class, sexuality, as well as issues of access and empowerment in terms of special learning needs and disability. These issues are fundamental to our society and so may need to be represented within the institutions' committee and communications structure. You might wish to consider how they are dealt with in your institution: for example, whether, and where, in your institution, there is student representation and/or support for students from black and/or minority ethnic groupings.

McNiff (1995) coined the phrase 'systems disadvantaged people'. She considers that, in many cases, the system of education provision is elitist. She begins by considering gender and disability, in particular, to introduce a critique of the education system and the 'silent systems of power' that control the management of education. This view is related to that held by conflict theorists, who see higher education as serving the needs and perpetuating the advantaged position of the elite. Ballantyne (1983) outlines both conflict and functionalist views of the higher education system. You might look at whether the present system of student representation encourages elitism: for instance, you could attempt to discover the extent to which all groups of students are appropriately represented in the various formal and informal institutional structures.

At Westminster College in Oxford, which has a Methodist foundation, a particularly effective voice comes from the staff of the theology department, who understand and are tolerant of religious difference. Societies exist for all the religious dimensions represented within the student body and arrangements are made for them to worship either in the college chapel or in rooms specifically set aside for particular religious groups. There is less interest in, and fewer special support or other arrangements for, men or students with disabilities, who are underrepresented in the student group within the college. You may wish to consider whether your institution has some systemic aspect of particular tolerance which allows students to continue to operate in a supportive and sympathetic environment.

RESEARCH TASK. FOCUS GROUP TECHNIQUES: SPECIAL CONSIDERATION GROUPS

Think of a particular group of students who you feel have been given some special consideration by your institution. Carry out an investigation into their perspectives and experiences as follows:

- Define your purposes and aims (for example, to discover whether the special provision being offered is considered adequate and how it could be tailored more closely to the needs and interests of the special interest group).
- Define your special consideration group (for example, potential students from a black and/or minority ethnic group).
- Define the characteristics of your group so that you take a representative sample from within the special consideration group.
- Select your sample (or samples if you wish to consider more than one grouping).
- Stimulate discussion in various ways. For instance you could:
  - get the students to write their perceptions of the situation on pieces of paper and stick them up on a wall.
  - ask students to select from a list of words or statements those with which they agree.
- The group should then be asked either to sort and group their comments, discussing groups of related comments, or to discuss their individual responses in order to identify areas where they agree and others where there is a variety of opinion.
- Take field notes of the words and phrases being used or tape the discussion that ensues. Do not intervene in the discussion until it begins to move away from the focus

You may wish to set up a grouping of staff at the institution and carry out the research task with them in order to ascertain their perceptions of the provision and some contrasting perspectives from two stakeholders in the education system.

For an outline of some of the potential advantages and disadvantages of group focus techniques, see Ashcroft et al. (1996).

Kelly and Slaughter (1991) found that there was a widespread lack of awareness within the educational system of equal opportunities issues and that, in particular, few departments had general policies on equal opportunities. Your interest may focus on a particular area of equal opportunities and some of these will now be considered briefly. (Issues of equal opportunities, and theoretical frameworks for their analysis in colleges and universities are discussed in some detail in Ashcroft et al., 1996.)

Disability

In the UK, for several years there has been a debate about the desirability of integrating students with disabilities into mainstream education provision. One view is that this is to the advantage of the students, providing them with the same opportunities as other students, and to society as a whole, in promoting tolerance and understanding. The other view considers this to be a ploy to obtain education on the 'cheap' for these students who require special facilities and extra attention. Within the primary and secondary education systems, the closing of special schools for those with special educational needs has placed an increasing burden on schools already struggling through lack of resources.

The debate about segregation versus integration and inclusion versus exclusion of students with special needs is by no means a straightforward one. In investigating the dilemmas that underpin potential resolutions within particular institutional contexts, it is important that you allow the voice of the student to be heard. The self-advocacy movement has as much to offer a consideration of the ethical issues in investigating the experiences of relatively powerless groups in society as it has to decisions about provision. It is important that researchers do not become part of the oppression that such students experience, by treating them as 'subjects' without expertise to offer in understanding their own disabilities and needs.

When researching the perspectives of the relatively powerless, it may be particularly important that *their* subjective experience is recorded, rather than yours. It may be appropriate to start with *their* ideas about what data should be collected and the best methods to use, and to finish with *their* interpretation of the data, rather than yours.

An important consideration in looking at the experiences of relatively disadvantaged groups in society are the assumptions as to where the 'problem' lies. For example, students with disabilities may be seen as 'owning' the problem, and therefore needing 'special' consideration. Alternatively, the 'problem' could be seem as residing in the normal organization and assumptions within an institution. Exclusion then becomes something that the institution has 'done', and so it must recognize it as institutional discrimination and attempt to justify it.

Some institutions turn away students with disabilities because their facilities are inadequate to meet their needs. Access is commonly cited as a reason for excluding students who use wheelchairs. If your institution accepts some categories of students with disabilities, for example, partially sighted students, you might want to consider how the needs of the student are being met. Students may need some particular piece of equipment such as an optical reader or tactile equipment to aid understanding or presentation. Ducker (1993) writes about the needs of visually impaired students in developing their graph drawing and other mathematical capabilities. However, it may be that staff attitudes and the institutional will to adapt organizational arrangements may be as important to achieving equality of opportunity for many students with disabilities as the availability of special equipment.

It is our experience that students are frequently taught in a variety of rooms spread throughout the campus, and it may be left to students with mobility problems to explain to staff their needs and to make arrangements for special equipment to be placed in the lecture room. For instance, a partially sighted student who is taught at one college has had an optical reader supplied by the college, but the onus is on her to see that the equipment is placed in the correct room prior to a lecture session. The college has a relatively small campus. Larger institutions may have many more students who require special facilities. It might be worth considering how their needs are served by the college administration, the extent to which it is ethically correct to give students with disabilities responsibility for organizing systems and equipment to meet their own needs, and how much normal channels of communication may need to be adapted to allow this to happen (for instance, to give the students some autonomy in decisions relating to the ordering of equipment).

HMSO (1995) sets out the government's objectives for ending discrimination against people with disabilities and includes a chapter on education. You might wish to consider how your institution is working to achieve these objectives.

RESEARCH TASK. GROUP INTERVIEW: PARENTAL INVOLVEMENT IN THE EDUCATION OF STUDENTS WITH DISABILITIES

SKILL (1993) sets out values and principles underpinning the setting up of parents' support groups within colleges. It looks at practical aspects, making recommendations for senior management and governors, and includes a number of case studies.

Consider the implications of this publication for students in your institution; whether parents are involved with the education of students and under what circumstances this is desirable:

- Ascertain the number of students with disabilities in your institution and the categories of disability.
- Identify the college's/university's policy or practice with regard to these students.
- Decide on your focus (for instance you might wish to focus on a specific area of disability or to consider the whole range as manifested in your institution).
- Set up interviews with a group of students.
- Carry out a group discussion to discover whether there is parental involvement and the form that it takes. For instance you could discover:
  - how often they see their parents;
  - whether their parents give them particular forms of help.

Make notes of:

- your value judgements during the process;
- your students' value judgements;
- whether particular types of disability seem to lead to more parental involvement;
- whether students appear to wish for more independence;
- the effect of financial considerations on this;
- the effect of the level support for the disability provided by the institution.

Where parents are involved, you may wish to interview them to ascertain their perspectives. You might integrate your findings with those from a more detailed look at the apparent effects of disability, and attitudes to it, on student autonomy; this might include observation, in-depth interviews, field notes and diaries.

Diaries and field notes allow you to collect a range of information as it occurs, using question and answer techniques with individuals or groups, observations, and so on, in order to analyse and interpret it at a later date (see for instance, Burgess, 1984, for suggestions on how to go about this). You could ask students or their parents to keep diaries.

Produce an initial paper outlining what you have found out and the issues raised for parental involvement and/or the right of students with disabilities to independence.

Race

Race is an area of investigation that requires particular sensitivity. It is important that you become familiar with the value positions espoused by integrationalists, those who believe in multicultural and inclusive education, and those who espouse anti-racist education. There are also issues about the language of debate. These issues and the theoretical frameworks that underpin them are looked at in more detail in Ashcroft *et al.* (1996).

Black and ethnic minority groups in the UK are becoming better represented in both the college and university sector, but the picture is uneven. Some groups appear to be over-represented and some, for instance men from Afro-Carribean backgrounds, are under-represented in higher level courses. Most institutions fail to reflect the racial mix of the society within which they are situated. Clay *et al.* (1995), in comparing Britain and the Netherlands, found that in the Netherlands in 1984/85 participation in higher education was lower than 2 per cent for black and ethnic minority groupings and pass rates were between 14 and 38 per cent. When it comes to looking at the particular subjects studied, the picture is even more uneven, with some subjects appearing particularly unattractive to members of black and ethnic minority groups. In Britain, with 4.7 per cent of the population belonging to black and ethnic minority groupings, only 2 per cent of students recruited onto Post-Graduate Certificate of Education courses belong to these groupings and there is a failure rate of 10 per cent.

An area for investigation might entail a comparison of different institutions, their racial composition and the reasons for a particular racial mix. It might be worth considering the differences between colleges and universities, since further education colleges are more likely to have students from the lower socio-economic backgrounds and there is sometimes a correlation between racial origins and socio-economic class. The *Higher Education Digest* (Quality Support Centre, 1996) describes the trends identified by the UK higher education admissions agency (UCAS) applications in 1991. It shows that 82 per cent of applicants are white, 13.5 per cent are from black and ethnic minority groupings and 4.5 per cent are unknown. These are home applicants and do not include overseas students, many of whom might belong to ethnic groupings. These figures give you a base-line to compare your institution's recruitment with the national percentages and with other institutions.

The UK Race Discrimination Act (1976) outlaws direct and indirect racial discrimination in institutions. However, within the field of higher education in the UK and the USA, there has been a great deal of controversy over the statements made recently by academics concerning the so-called 'genetic inferiority of blacks'. Consider the case of Christopher Brand, a lecturer at Edinburgh University and author of a book on race and ability that was recently withdrawn from publication. The book was, according to the publishers John Wiley a 'well written, argued, critical review'. However, Brand subsequently expanded his views on race and the publishers withdrew the book on the grounds that they were unable to agree with the racist views expressed in the interview. The students at Edinburgh University have taken action and refused to be taught by this lecturer, voting to have him removed from his teaching responsibilities. The incident points to a tension between academic freedom and equality of opportunity. We would argue, along with most student associations, that no publication platform should be given to racists and fascists.

In the UK, most institutions have equal opportunities policies that outlaw racism. Where racism exists, it is likely to be subtle rather than blatant and often results from institutional inertia rather than intent. Institutions which do not take action to eliminate this subtle form of discrimination may fail to recruit many students from black and ethnic minority groupings. Siraj-Blatchford (1991) found that 'personal and institutional racism experienced by potential trainees and recruits are crucial determinants in poor recruitment and retention rates'. Her study of teacher education identified racism in the accommodation offered to black and ethnic minority students, in course content, administration and work placements as well as interpersonal racism from both staff and students.

Sometimes racism appears to exist within the normal day-to-day organizational and social arrangements of an institution. In these circumstances, institutional racism may be described by the college or university authorities as a 'problem' of the black community who have difficulties adjusting to the institution. Some black students may indeed find it difficult to make the change from home to university. We are aware of a situation where a very able black student had real difficulties in adapting to the change when moving from a mainly black community in an inner London borough, to living in a mainly white community, where many of the other students had affluent parents who supported them totally as they moved through college. For this student, parental support was not a possibility and she has had to work at evenings and weekends to get through the course. Even more traumatic was the cultural change, the realization that there were different cultural values, to which the black student had real difficulty in relating.

Students in these circumstances may need help and support. The most important thing to realize here is that the 'problem' is that of the institution, not of the students. It is the institution that must adapt. The institution may need to take special measures to support black students directly in helping to set up mutual support groups. We may also need to ensure that students are not experiencing direct or indirect discrimination and that the curriculum is not Euro-centric in its orientation.

Racism is a difficult area to research. Finding out if our own or our colleague's actions are racially discriminating must be done with great sensitivity. One method of preventing the feelings of threat that direct enquiry into respondents' behaviour and attitudes might cause is to use scenario analysis. It is also essential that you identify and give 'voice' to the dominated group themselves (Siraj-Blatchford, 1994).

You may find it easier to focus on the effects of racism within documentary sources or other records, rather than on reports on actual or hypothetical individuals: for instance, as indicated by low recruitment figures.

RESEARCH TASK. DOCUMENT SEARCH AND INTERVIEWS: COURSE MATERIALS

Analyse course offerings within your institution to discover whether they exhibit *either* an anti-racist *or* multicultural perspective (see Ashcroft et al., 1996, for more detail on these perspectives).

Collect course outlines available within your institution and carry out the following:

- Sort the courses into those which have adopted an anti-racist or multicultural perspective and those which you feel have given little thought to the issues (see Blackburn, 1996, outlining the case for ethnic diversity to be inspected by OFSTED).
- Identify those courses that have taken up the opportunity to enrich themselves in this way.
- With the support of black and ethnic minority colleagues or students, carry out a detailed analysis of the ways in which this has been achieved (for instance: through discussion of student attitudes; concern to adopt the use of inclusive language in the teaching process; the provision of overseas visits; visits to religious orders from other cultures; invitations to visitors from other cultures).
- Identify the areas for future development.

Return to the courses that have yet to take up the challenge. With great sensitivity:

- ascertain from colleagues the reason for the non-inclusion of anti-racist or multicultural perspectives in the programme;
- classify these reasons (for instance, lack of expertise, lack of awareness of the possibilities).

> Write a paper for your institution, identifying areas of good practice in anti-racist *or* multicultural education and making suggestions as to how barriers to good practice might be avoided. Focus on the positive: take care to protect the anonymity of individuals or programmes where good practice is absent or underdeveloped.

Gender

Gender is an area that has been relatively well researched. The issues here are manifold: the gender balance on different types of courses; the ratio of women to men in senior positions within institutions; and the sexual harassment of staff and students. Stiver Lie *et al.* (1994) have gathered a number of contributions which focus on the gender gap in education across the world.

An interesting focus for research is the career aspirations of female students. There has been a change in the balance of male and female students between the 1960s and the 1990s. In the 1960s, 25 per cent of students were female; in 1994 that figure has risen to 51.7 per cent. (Leckey *et al.*, 1995). With respect to career aspirations and gender, they state that females are present in much higher numbers on courses concerned with the social sciences, humanities and education. You might investigate the amount of time and the quality of attention those running these courses and the students within them appear give to considering occupational aspirations and the employment attitudes of female and male students.

Gutek and Larwood (1987) found that there are three fundamental differences between males and females when considering career aspirations. These are differing expectations of the jobs they are about to do, differing patterns of parenting, and discrimination and stereotyping of females in the workplace into specific roles.

Dey and Hurtado (1995), researching in the USA, found that there is an increase in the number of female students opting to do 'traditionally' male courses such as law, medicine and physical sciences.

At Westminster College, which has a large cohort training to be teachers in primary schools, it would appear to be the case that male students, even those who have performed poorly throughout the course, find a position much more quickly than female students. Men are under-represented in primary schools and in infant classrooms especially. You might look at whether this acts as an advantage when it comes to shortlisting and interviews, and whether women who apply for work in traditionally male occupations enjoy a similar advantage. At the University of the West of England, Foster (1995) investigated the experiences of male students on a similar course and found that, although male students appear to find a post more quickly than females, the situation is more complex than it appears at first. She found that male students on a traditionally female course are privileged in some ways, but also experience some discrimination.

RESEARCH TASK. QUESTIONNAIRE:COMPARISON OF MALE AND FEMALE JOB OPPORTUNITIES

Prepare your questionnaire as follows:

- Define precisely those aspects of male and female job opportunities in which you are particularly interested (for example, the correlation between job opportunities and gender in a particular area).
- Define exactly what you want to know about that area (for example, student's final qualifications, date of first application, date of first interview, number of interviews, and date of appointment).
- Decide on your target population (for example, a cross-section of all students, a particular target group, such as students who come to the institution straight from school/from Access courses, etc).
- Decide on the format for the questions for your survey (for example, closed, semantic differential, multiple choice).
- Interview some of your target population to check that the issues that you have identified are the salient ones from their point of view.
- Design questions that will elicit the information in which you are interested.
- Test the questions on a small sub-set of your target group – ask them to comment on how easy the questions are to understand, whether they are ambiguous, whether their interpretation of the information corresponds with yours; whether their interpretation of the meanings of particular responses corresponds with yours.
- Refine you questionnaire in the light of this feedback.

For further information on questionnaires, their advantages and the types of questions to use see Chapter 3, and for ways that you might analyse the data see Bennett *et al.* (1996).

Class

As the opportunities for completing a course with an adequate grant diminish in the UK, class is increasingly becoming an issue. The effect of the reduction of the mandatory grant on recruitment from lower socio-economic groups might be a fruitful area for research. The notion of class is inextricably tied up with the function of higher education. Any view of class will be influenced by whether you take a functionalist, Marxist or an interpretative perspective of the system. Functionalists and Marxists take a macro view of society and the education system, while interpretative approaches take more micro/interactional perspectives.

If you decide to carry out an analysis of class issues in education, you may need to clarify your personal perspective and how it relates to each of the above theories, in order to rationally present your own views and research. Blackledge and Hunt (1985) present each of these theories and their relationship to education; another excellent starting point is provided by Burrell and Morgan (1980).

The statistics in the *Higher Education Digest* (Quality Support Centre, 1996) show that, in the UK, more applicants from the lower social classes choose to remain in their home region. In socio-economic class five, almost 60 per cent choose to remain, while in socio-economic class one, about 35 per cent choose to remain. The total student body, represented by home applications, has 52 per cent students from classes one and two and the remaining students fall into categories three to five. Only 2 per cent of students come from socio-economic class category five.

RESEARCH TASK. COMPARISON OF SOCIO-ECONOMIC CLASS CATEGORIES FOR DIFFERING INSTITUTIONS

In conjunction with another institution. set up a comparison of the socio-economic class structure of your institutions as follows:

- Collect data on the class origins of your students. (You will usually be able to find this data through the Application Clearing House information.) Students who have come straight from their parental home will have a class attributed to them by virtue of their principal wage-earning parent's occupation. Mature students who have worked prior to attending a course will have a class attributed to them by virtue of their previous employment.
- Compare the data in relation to the other institutions taking part in the survey.
- Consider the similarities and differences outlined by the data (for instance, whether colleges or universities have a higher proportion of these students).
- Undertake unstructured interviews with staff within your institution about the data emerging from your analysis.

- From these interviews identify issues that you will explore through open-ended questions with a wider sample.
- Test your questions on your original sample to check how easy they are to understand and whether they are ambiguous; your interpretation of their meanings, and so on (see the previous research task).
- Set up semi-structured interviews to ascertain explanations for the trends identified in your data.

Write a paper relating your results to one of the main theoretical frameworks mentioned above.

Sexual Orientation

Despite the opening up of society over the last two decades and the lessening of intolerance, sexual orientation is still a highly emotional issue for many people. Some reject the notion of prejudice about homosexuality. Others still uncritically equate gay and lesbian members of our society with paedophiles and sex offenders. Any investigation of these attitudes clearly requires sensitivity to the personal and political issues. Many common assumptions may be grossly offensive to those stigmatized as 'abnormal'. You could look at whether particular attitudes are related to a notion of sexual orientation as innate or the view that we are all fundamentally bisexual and that sexual responses and practices are learned through socialization.

To those who subscribe to the latter position, the issue is not only about appropriate role models, rounded and complete curricula and so on, but also about power. There is evidence that homosexuality can be a barrier to educational success. Khayatt (1994) found that secondary-age children who were, or believed they might be, homosexual, often had to endure taunts and uncertainties that sometimes led them to drop out of school or to be expelled. You could investigate whether gay, lesbian and bisexual students in your institution experience a similar lack of support, misinformation or silence about their sexuality.

Epstein (1994) points out that in the UK during the 1980s, a concern for the feelings of gay and lesbian students became associated with 'loony left-wing' policies in education. Outside of education, there is a growth of community-based information and support groups and, increasingly, the celebration of sexual diversity. You could look at whether students find their sources of support outside the institution. Where this is the case, research into the student experience may be particularly difficult, since you may face problems in identifying and negotiating access to a representative sample of students. As in the case of other forms of oppression, we strongly advise any member of the dominant group (in this case, heterosexuals) who are considering research in the area to find a group or individual homosexual with whom to collaborate and share the analysis.

Many institutions, such as Bath University, have societies and support groups for gay and lesbian students. These can help students at a time when some may be experiencing uncertainty, fear and (with the advent of HIV and AIDS) the loss of friends or loved ones. Meredeen (1988) discusses the difficulties for students who may know about or suspect their sexual preference for the same sex but as yet have not been able to 'come out'. It is suggested that it is important for students to join societies, where they exist, so as to have opportunities to discuss their thoughts and concerns and to combat feelings of being the 'odd one out'.

RESEARCH TASK. COMPARISON OF PROVISION FOR GAY, BISEXUAL AND LESBIAN STUDENTS

Contact the student union within a number of institutions.

Construct a questionnaire that will allow you to discover the following information from the student unions:

- whether or not societies or support groups exist in those institutions for gay or lesbian students;
- whether societies exist at neighbouring institutions where gay or lesbian students may attend meetings;
- whether there are any other types of support mechanisms for gay or lesbian students;
- the number of students who belong to these societies where they exist;
- whether the institution has any policies which encompass the needs of gay or lesbian students and in particular ensures acceptance and respect for the individual needs of these students.

Check your questionnaire with an experienced researcher and a few gay, lesbian or bisexual students and/or colleagues. Refine your questionnaire in the light of their response.

Ask for details of any policies that exist be sent to you.

Use the resulting data as a starting point for an investigation into the needs of gay and lesbian students within your own institution.

Student Union Representation on Committees

In most UK institutions, the bulk of student representatives are elected through the student union. These representatives operate on many different levels and each student union will have its own internal structure. Below we consider a particular structure which operates at the University of the West of England and the impact the students can have in terms of their representation on specific committees within the university. This provides a basis for comparison and for identifying some of the issues.

The Structure of Student Support at the University of the West of England

Union Council	Governing body of the student union. All elected posts are accountable to the union committee. All policy decisions must be approved by the union committee, as must all constitutional changes. Union council representatives are elected onto the institution's major committees.
Executive Committee	Responsible for the day-to-day running of the union, including implementing policy, and make up of sabbatical and non-sabbatical posts. Non-sabbatical includes all the equal opportunities posts.
Site Committee	The institution is spread over five sites and each campus has its own committee of elected posts. The site committee has the same posts as the executive committee and thus is a lower tier with the same responsibilities with respect to their site.

There are thus three levels at which students can participate, either in terms of seeking or providing representation. The system operates when an issue is identified at site level and is taken up by the site committee. The representative from the site committee who sits on the executive committee takes the issue forward for further discussion and, if considered worthy, a proposal for action is drafted for the union council. At the union council this may be passed as a new policy and implemented.

The union council membership also forms the representatives on other major committees in the institution such as Academic Board, Academic Standards and Quality Group, Credit Accumulation and

Transfer Scheme Group, as well as the various faculty boards and sub-boards. These students attempt to represent the views of the student body rather than their own. The president of the student union also sits on the institution's Board of Governors. Your institution may be smaller, or operate on one site. It may be interesting to consider similarities and differences between various institutions.

RESEARCH TASK. STUDENT REPRESENTATION AND THE WORKINGS OF COMMITTEES

- Collect information on the structures for student representation from a number of institutions which differ in size.
- Interview students and managers within your own institution about their perceptions of how the structure works (for instance, the mechanisms for identifying areas of concern, the sort of input that is sought or given at academic committees where there is representation).
- Analyse the pattern of representation of students from various of the groupings outlined in this chapter.
- Identify whether:
  - certain groups are under-represented;
  - mechanisms for getting under-represented groups incorporated into the structure exist.

Use your data as the basis of a paper about the workings of the student representative system in various institutions and their relationship to the empowerment of groups traditionally under-represented at managerial levels in colleges and universities.

You could analyse the data you obtain by reference to theories of organizations. Barnard (1938) puts forward theories about decisions in organizations and outlines the types of decisions that occur in terms of the person involved and the organization. Scott (1992) considers three systems that organizations operate: rational, natural or open. Silverman (1970) considers there are three 'typologies of organizations': environment-input, environment-output, and a typology based on intra-organizational factors.

As well as the degree of student representation changing during the period from the mid-1980s to the mid-1990s, the level of student campaigning has also changed quite dramatically. Cawkwell and Pilkington (1994) consider not only the changes in students' rights and representation but also a range of related issues. In the 1960s there was little student representation and this caused many protests.

Another consideration is the weight given to the input of student representatives on institutional and union committees within particular types of institutions. Students representing their peers may only attend three meetings a year. The validity of their representation and their qualifications may be questioned by fellow students those with the oversight of the day-to-day running of the institution, who may wish or need to retain the real control. You might look at the purposes the student representatives actually serve; the extent to which the various participants in committee processes find students' influence to be real; whether they see it as a means to placate external evaluators (in the case of the institution) or whether they see it as giving the impression of democracy (in the case of student unions).

Those students who sit on committees may be intended to be representative of their peers. You could look at how (or whether) representation occurs when decisions or comments are called for within the context of a meeting. You could discover by what means the students themselves ensure views are representative, for instance discussing committee items within a forum of the union prior to the meeting.

RESEARCH TASK. SEMI-STRUCTURED INTERVIEWS: REPRESENTATION FROM STUDENTS' PERSPECTIVES

Carry out a semi-structured interview with a number of student representatives at your institution. You will need to define clearly some main headings for your questions:

● the representation;
● the method of selection for the representation;
● the parameters under which the representation is carried out;
● what contributions representatives have made within the committee forums;
● whether/how these vary from the committee structures within the union;
● what preparation they have had for representation;
● what preparation they would like to have;
● what they would suggest as minimal training for the role.

Sit in on a number of institutional and student union committees and observe the roles and contributions of student representatives and the reaction of staff members and chairs of the committees.

Use your results as the starting point for a paper on the roles and influence of student representation in committees within an institution.

In this chapter various issues linked to equality of opportunity and student representation have been considered. The intention has been to give the reader interested in this area a basis from which to move forward. The purpose has been to expose some of the current problems and policies that exist, in order to stimulate further research.

Annotated Reading List

Lovell, T and Leicester, M (1993) 'Gender and higher education', *Journal of Further Education and Higher Education,* 17, 1, Spring.
Research which shows that the evaluation of academic abilities and performance is carried out in situations which are problematical because they evidence a lack of awareness of equal opportunities at departmental level.

Lovell, T and Leicester, M (1994) 'Equal opportunities and university practice; race, gender and disability: a comparative perspective', *Journal of Further Education and Higher Education,* 18, 2.
Comparative analysis of data arising from a survey of equal opportunities practice in relation to race, gender and disability.

Standing Committee on Human Rights (1994) *Disability: An assessment of the implications of physical and sensory disability in the N. Ireland context together with supporting research papers,* London: HMSO.
Research into physical and sensory disability in Northern Ireland.

References

Ashcroft K, Bigger, C and Coates, D (1996) *Researching into Equal Opportunities in Colleges and Universities,* London: Kogan Page.

Ballantyne, J (1983) *The Sociology of Education,* Englewood Cliffs, NJ: Prentice-Hall.

Barnard, C I (1938) 'Decisions in organisations', in Castles, F C, Murray, D J and Pottor, D C eds, 1971) *Decisions, Organisations and Society,* Harmondsworth: Penguin.

Bennett, C, Higgins, C and Foreman-Peck, L (1996) *Researching into Teaching Methods in Colleges and Universities,* London: Kogan Page.

Blackburn, L (1996) 'Bid to end black history anomaly', *Times Educational Supplement,* 31 May 1996.

Blackledge, D and Hunt, B (1985) *Sociological Interpretations of Education,* Beckenham: Croom Helm.

Burgess, R (1984) 'Keeping a research diary', in Bell, J and Goulding, S (eds) *Conducting Small Scale Investigations in Education Management,* London: Harper and Row.

Burrell, G and Morgan, G (1980) *Sociological Paradigms and Organisational Analysis,* Aldershot: Gower.

Cawkwell, J and Pilkington, P (1994) 'Rights and Representation' in Haselgrove, S (ed.) *The Student Experience,* Buckingham: SRHE and Open University Press.

Clay, J, Cole, M and George, R (1995) 'Visible minority ethnic representation in teaching and teacher education in Britain and the Netherlands: some observations', *Journal of Further Education and Higher Education,* 19, 2, Summer.

Connolly, F M and Clandinin, D J (1990) 'Stories of experience and narrative enquiry', *Educational Researcher,* 19, 5, 214.

Cortazzi, M (1993) *Narrative Analysis,* London: Falmer Press.

Dey, E and Hurtado, S (1995) 'College impact, student impact: a reconsideration of the role of students within American higher education', *Higher Education,* 30, 2, September.

Ducker, L (1993) 'Visually impaired students drawing graphs', *Mathematics Teaching,* September.

Epstein, D (ed.) (1994) *Challenging Lesbian and Gay Inequalities in Education,* Buckingham: Open University Press.

Foster, T (1995) 'You don't have to be female to succeed on this course, but it helps', *The Redland Papers,* 3, 35–42.

Gutek, B and Larwood, L (1987) *Women's Career Development,* Beverley Hills, CA: Sage.

HMSO (1995) *Ending Discrimination Against Disabled People,* London: HMSO.

Kelly, G and Slaughter, S A (1991) *Women's Higher Education in Comparative Perspective,* Dordrecht: Kluwer.

Khayatt, D (1994) 'Surviving school as a lesbian student', *Gender and Education,* 6, 1, 47–62.

Leckey, J, McGuigan, M and Harrison, R (1995) 'Career aspirations and expectations: does gender matter?', *Journal of Further Education and Higher Education,* 19, 2, Summer.

Meredeen, S (1988) *Study for Survival and Success. Guidenotes for college students,* London: Paul Chapman.

McNiff, J (1995) 'Systems disadvantaged people – a case for shifting responsibility', *Action Researcher,* 4, Autumn.

Quality Support Centre (1996) 'Progression into higher education: current trends', *Higher Education Digest,* Open University.

Scott, W R (1992) *Organisations' Rational, Natural and Open Systems,* London: Prentice Hall.

Silverman, D (1970) *The Theory of Organisations: A sociological framework,* Oxford: Heinemann.

Siraj-Blatchford, I (1991) 'A study of black students' perception of racism in ITE', *British Educational Research Journal,* 17, 1.

Siraj-Blatchford, I (1994) *Praxis Makes Perfect,* Nottingham: Education Now.

SKILL: National Bureau for Students with Disabilities (1993) *Setting up Parents' Support Groups in FE Colleges,* London: SKILL.

Stiver Lie, S, Malik, L and Harris, D (1994) *The Gender Gap in Higher Education World Yearbook of Education 1994,* London: Kogan Page.

Chapter 5

Teaching and Learning in Colleges and Universities

In Chapter 2 we began asking some fairly fundamental questions about the aims and objectives of colleges and universities. We argued that the institutions' stated aims and objectives provide important insights into the expectations that both students and lecturers/tutors are likely to bring with them into the seminar room and lecture theatre. As we also argued, these aims constitute important institutional contexts that any research project will need to be either set within or engaged upon. In addition to contributing towards the introduction and literature review in your research report, these documentary analyses will inform your analysis throughout the study.

We move away from the macro-institutional contexts now to focus more closely on learning and teaching practices. In recent years, the study of these practices in education has most generally become the subject of 'curriculum studies'. As Carr (1993) has noted, this is an area of educational scholarship that is concerned with three distinct aspects:

- the underlying aims and values that inform the selection of curriculum content;
- the theories of knowledge that underlie the way that content is organized;
- the pedagogical principles that underlie the way the contents are taught, learned and assessed.

The Curriculum

Curriculum studies often provide theoretical accounts that describe teaching and learning as a socially constructed and historically evolving cultural product. These accounts also show that our practices are being continually constructed and reconstructed in a complex process of contest and struggle between the demands of the various institutional interest groups, and between individual tutors and their students. Curriculum studies also show how these different views ultimately reflect alternative perceptions of what constitutes 'good practice' and ultimately what would constitute a 'good society'.

A number of approaches to both the curriculum and curriculum studies are possible. Grundy (1987) has identified three major approaches adopted in the literature: the conceptual, cultural and critical. These three approaches may be considered as corresponding to:

- the kind of social history approach adopted by Goodson (1983);
- the sociology of knowledge/critical ideological perspective adopted by educational sociologists such as Apple (1979), Giroux (1992) and Young (1970);
- the liberal cultural and philosophical analysis of Lawton (1989).

Although the terms that are adopted here may seem off-putting, a great deal can be learnt from studies in each of these traditions. In particular, the sociology of education has contributed a good deal to our understanding of curriculum in general. The term 'hidden curriculum' has been used to refer to the often unintentional consequences of particular curricular practices and this has been especially valuable in the context of studies concerned with gender equality in schooling. A parallel concept of 'institutional racism' has been employed in race equality research. Much of the work conducted in the sociology of education in recent years has been particularly concerned with issues surrounding:

- social stratification and bias;
- economic and cultural reproduction;
- student mediation, resistance and empowerment.

While these may not be of direct concern in your present study, you should be aware that the work conducted in these areas may still be relevant to you, if your study relates to any kind of conflict situation. An example might be the struggle between different departments in the formation of a faculty, or the various ways that a particular curriculum package has been implemented to satisfy the conflicting needs of different groups of lecturers and students. In either case, the chances are that it will be the sociologists (and very possibly the more radical ones) who have provided the best tools for your analysis.

In an introductory text of this sort, we can do little more than point out the general directions that your study might take. Later, we will take a look at some of the ways that the processes of teaching and learning, the pedagogic elements of curriculum practice, may be studied. Before then, we shall consider the benefits to be gained form implementing some form of discourse analysis in the study of curriculum content.

Discourse Analysis

Discourse analysis involves a number of methodological approaches but each has been applied to investigate what van Dijk (1985) has referred to as, 'the many dimensions of text, talk, and their cognitive, social and cultural contexts'. As Banister *et al.* (1994, p.92) put it:

> Discourse analysis treats the social world as a text, or rather as a system of texts which can be systematically 'read' by a researcher to lay open the psychological processes that lie within them, processes that the discipline of psychology usually attributes to a machinery inside the individual's head.

In linguistics, discourse analysis has referred to the study of linguistic effects such as semantics (stylistic and syntactic) where textual description takes into account sentence sequences as well as sentence structure. A thorough discussion of the more radical contemporary approaches to discourse analysis is beyond the scope of this text. However, a few words about two of the most interesting variants will at least provide readers with some references to follow up. A very brief introduction to 'deconstructionism' and 'ideological analysis' therefore follows.

Deconstructionism

The term 'deconstruction' is normally associated with the work of the post-structuralist Derrida (1967). Sarup (1988, p.56) provides a helpful account of the kind of methodological processes involved:

> Deconstructive 'close-reading', having 'interrogated' the text, breaks through its defences and shows that a set of binary oppositions can be found 'inscribed' within it. In each of the pairs, private/public, masculine/feminine, same/other, rational/ irrational, true/false, central/peripheral, etc, the first term is privileged. Deconstructors show that the privileged term depends for its identity on its excluding the other and demonstrates that primacy really belongs to the subordinate term instead.

Because it rejects the notion that texts can be considered to possess any internal structure, logic or meaning, deconstructionalism is often referred to as a post-structuralist theoretical framework. It is grounded upon a radical acceptance of the self-referenciality of linguistic forms and therefore, ultimately, the practice can only result in infinite regress. The process does, however, provide us with a means of questioning commonly accepted practices and meanings.

By contrast, Foucault's (1969) form of discourse analysis has focused on broader fields of study such as 'medical perception'. His work has provided what he terms an 'archaeology' of common discourses such as 'madness and civilization', 'sexuality' and 'discipline and punishment'. Throughout his work, Foucault has been interested in the ways in which discourses have been classified and represented over time. In his later work, he identified the principle by which power has come to be increasingly exercised through surveillance. His notion of panopticism has been used as a model in a wide range of subsequent studies. The 'panopticon' was an architectural device first advocated by Bentham at the end of the 18th century. As applied to prison populations, the prisoners were to be housed in a circular arrangement of cells all open to observation from a central watch tower or guard room. As the prisoners could never be certain that they were not being watched from the panopticon, they gradually came to police their own behaviour. According to Foucault (1977), similar principles came to be employed to control the rest of the population, first in schools, barracks and hospitals and then more generally through the establishment of legal and financial dossiers, systems of assessment and classification.

A number of different forms of domination are undoubtedly realized through such processes of surveillance and you may be able to identify particular aspects of your own study that would fit this model. In any event, you will almost certainly be able to identify particular discourses that have been sustained over time within your subject of study. These may, in turn, be related to even broader discourses. For example, a number of studies in the 1980s located their analysis of institutional changes in 'Thatcherism'. This in turn could be related to economic and social evolutionary ideas that date back to the 19th century. One of the most important insights that discourse analysis, and perhaps Foucault's work in particular, has provided is the recognition that discourses often function to close off the possibilities for practical change. Within any discourse, there are things that may not be said or thought. In providing a ready-made way of thinking about something, discourses may be considered to act ideologically to rule out alternative ways of thinking and also to preserve the current distribution of power.

For the purposes of the sort of initial studies that we envisage our readers carrying out, a simplified version of the kind of ideological analysis suggested by Cormack (1992) will be offered as a form of deconstruction.

Ideological analysis

In choosing to adopt the term 'ideology' here, we are aware of the special difficulties of definition. The word has been applied in a variety of ways and has often been used *and abused* to refer to both negative and hidden ideas and assumptions. Such applications have a long history, yet the word's most common uses today are often with reference to the ideological commitments of 'idealists' or to beliefs that are implicitly false or distorted. For the purposes of this discussion, we wish to distance ourselves from such narrow definitions. We have adopted the term for want of a better one, and we adopt it here according to its widest sociological definition, to refer to *any* set of associated beliefs, attitudes and opinions held by individuals or groups. From this perspective, we consider that we all have sets of beliefs, most of which we share as common knowledge with significant people around us.

RESEARCH TASK. IDEOLOGICAL DECONSTRUCTION

To begin you will need a subject for the ideological analysis. Cultural products such as policies and curriculum documents would provide suitable subjects, but you may wish to focus on an event such as 'a tutorial', 'a seminar' or 'the block lecture' instead. Ask the following key questions:

- How is the subject matter organized?
- What educational purposes does it serve?
- What learning outcomes is it intended to achieve?
- By what methods are such outcomes to be evaluated?
- How has it developed historically?
- What are the implicit views of 'good practice' or the 'good society' that are reflected in it?

Cormack (1992) provides another five categories of analysis which could serve as a checklist for your own studies:

- Content
  - what obvious beliefs/values are involved
  - what language/terminology is used (and what are the implications of this)
  - what stereotypes can be identified.

- Structure
  - are textual examples closely related to policy or curriculum statements – is there ideological closure (the final word)? Note: research tends to 'crop' reality as we cannot possibly look at everything or anything from every direction at the same time!
  - are binary oppositions being employed? Many feminists argue (we think correctly) that the tendency to always define problems in binary terms is inherently sexist, aggressive and hierarchical.
- Absence
  - most importantly, what is it that the text is claiming to represent and does it do so?
- Style
  - are contentious matters being presented as factual and objective?
- Mode of address
  - who is it written for?
  - do all of those who have an intersect in the matter have access?

Pedagogy: Providing Opportunities for Students to Learn

As Brown and Atkins (1988) have suggested, the various methods of teaching may be placed on a continuum (see Figure 5.1). At one extreme is the formal lecture in which student control and participation is usually minimal. This method benefits from economies of scale and can be achieved in large lecture theatres or even through radio, video or television. Although students have no control over the content, they do have a degree of choice concerning the aspects they wish to note. In a live lecture, they may choose to ask questions. Where lectures have been recorded, they may select particular areas of special interest. Similarly, in private study where the lecturer's participation and control may be considered minimal, a hidden structure may be provided by the particular questions being addressed and the selection of texts made available.

You will undoubtedly be able to place your own favoured teaching method somewhere along this continuum. It is not the concern of this book to discuss the relative merits of the various approaches but it would seem reasonable to assume that each has its own advantages and drawbacks and that selection might best be considered in terms of 'fitness for purpose'. That being the case, the problem becomes one of analysing your own particular needs and perhaps experimenting to find the most effective method. Brown and Atkins (1988) provide some excellent guidance in this area; readers may also wish to refer to Ashcroft and Foreman-Peck (1994).

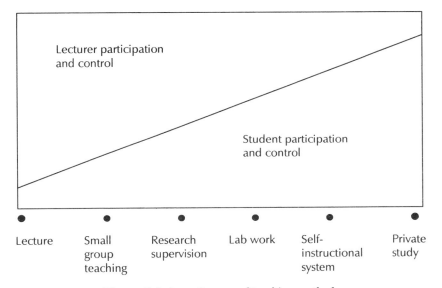

Lecturer participation and control

Student participation and control

| Lecture | Small group teaching | Research supervision | Lab work | Self-instructional system | Private study |

Figure 5.1 *A continuum of teaching methods*

Symbolic Interactionism

One of the most important criteria for determining the effectiveness of a particular teaching style is how the students respond and learn in the environment that you have created. One approach to analysing this is 'symbolic interactionism'. This provides a radical alternative to the suggestion that the actions of individuals and groups are passive or determined by psychological attributes such as drives, attitudes and personalities. This perspective also rejects theoretical alternatives that would over-emphasize the determining effects of external structures such as class, race or gender. Symbolic interactionists consider the socially determined and social determining 'self' to be essentially recip-rocal. Symbolic interactionists explain the action of individuals through reference to their interactions with those 'significant others' around them. Individuals are seen as active in accepting, modifying and resisting the influence of others. As Cohen and Manion (1994) have suggested, these models have often been considered to 'fit' quite naturally with the kind of concentrated action found in classrooms and schools, where pupils and teachers are 'continually adjusting, reckoning, evaluating, bargaining, acting and changing' (Woods, 1979).

Arguably, the approach is equally relevant in colleges and universities where there may be a stronger tradition of taking seriously the interpretations and subjective understanding of the teaching and learning processes held by our students. The interpretations and understandings that guide our students' actions are not always entirely conscious and so we cannot simply ask them to tell us about them. Our students are constantly engaged in a process of interpretation and definition as they move from one situation to another. As Tesch (1990, p.83) suggests:

> The researcher has to infer the salient features of this operation by collecting all kinds of data (by interviewing, examining personal documents, but particularly by observing) and then extracting from these records the material that is relevant to the question the researcher asks.

RESEARCH TASK. SYMBOLIC INTERACTIONISM

- Set up a video recorder in your teaching room and record a lecture or seminar. If the video has a time-elapsed display, use it, as it will be helpful in your analysis.
- Play back the recording, collating the data of particular concern. These areas provide your initial 'anticipatory data reduction' categories. As the research progresses they will become more clearly defined and differentiated.
- Your notes at this stage will probably take the form of summary descriptions of a series of separate 'incidents'. Mark each incident with a number that relates it to one of the relevant concerns/categories and index it against the time it occurred. For example, you may be keen to note each time the students ask questions and each time they redirect the discussion in some way, so you might code (categorize) each question '1' and each redirection '2'.
- Try to identify phenomena that tend to appear simultaneously, for example, increased student participation – categories 1 and 2, and references made to student experience – category 3.
- Try to form some tentative propositions (for example, the students are more inclined to participate when the discussion centres on events that they have experienced themselves).
- Systematically go through your recording to see if the events that have prompted the development of the tentative proposition are typical and widespread.

● Use the concrete data to confirm, disconfirm or modify the proposition and to present your findings.

As Becker and Geer (1982, p.243) suggest, you should also look for 'negative cases' whose lack would assure the validity of the 'perspective' offered. The findings may be:

> presented as a set of statements about 'the necessary and sufficient conditions for the existence of some phenomenon', statements that some phenomenon is an 'important' or 'basic' element in the organisation, or 'statements identifying a situation as an instance of some process or phenomenon described more abstractly in sociological theory

Reflecting Upon Your Own Teaching Practice

A major educational research question in recent years has been how to understand the relationship between our theory and practice. Winter's (1991) answer has been that education is always both theoretical practice and practical theory. In many ways, your choice of research methodology will be determined by the personal aims that you have for your research. You will need to ask yourself whether it is intended to 'reveal the truth' in some way; are you concerned with 'theory'; or do you want your study to inform practice directly.

If your concern is with the latter you might consider adopting the principles of 'reflective practice' that have become a central feature of teacher education courses in recent years. Implicit in the notion of the trainee teacher as a 'reflective practitioner' is the idea of the student following an ongoing critical evaluative process of classroom management, curriculum and pedagogic development.

Given that this ongoing commitment to critical reflection is strongly encouraged in school teachers, it seems only reasonable that it should also apply to tutors. In fact the notion of the 'reflective practitioner' has a great deal to offer lecturers in colleges and universities in general. While there may have been little attention given to the quality of teaching in further and higher education in the past this is certainly a major concern today.

In fact, the concept of 'action research' that we discussed earlier and 'reflective practice' are closely related. To conduct action research and to reflectively practice, one plans, acts, observes, collects data and reflects on that action and data. In either case, as Elliot (1991, pp.49–50) has argued: 'The reflective practitioner's understanding of the values (s)he attempts to realise in practice are continually transformed in the process of reflecting about such attempts'.

As it happens, the values that have been applied by reflective educators in practice have often been criticized for their essentially 'regulative' nature. There is a risk, in any form of practitioner research, of following narrowly defined professional interests (Siraj-Blatchford,1993; Weiner, 1989). When we are involved in action research and reflective practice, our reflections need to be informed by principles of 'critical enquiry'. As was mentioned in Chapter 1, in their discussion of the needs of reflective students, a number of writers (for instance, Ashcroft and Griffiths, 1989) have referred to three particular attitudes and values that need to be addressed:

- Open-mindedness – a willingness to actively seek out other perspectives.
- Commitment – the wholehearted acceptance of such open-minded responsibility in one's personal and professional life.
- Responsibility – a willingness to consider the broad, long-term, political and social consequences as well as the narrow, short-term and professional consequences of any action.

It will only be through accepting these attitudes and values ourselves that we can ensure that we avoid a narrow-minded, regulative approach in our own studies.

Open-mindedness implies that you are willing to seek out and investigate the perspectives of others who have an interest in the education process; not to unthinkingly accept their positions, but rather to evaluate them in the light of your values and experience.

Responsibility implies that you seek evidence of the effects of your actions and values, and those of others, on each of the legitimate stakeholders in education. The research task below is designed to enable you to put these notions of open-mindedness and responsibility into some sort of practice.

RESEARCH TASK. EXPLORING IMPLICIT THEORIES OF EDUCATION

Choose one of the courses on which you teach. List all the people or groups of people who you think are the stakeholders of that course (for instance, funders, students, parents, employers, institutional managers, other lecturers). Ask yourself why they might have an interest in the course.

Ask some of your stakeholders the following two questions. Try to ensure that you talk with at least one representative from each category of stakeholder (you may need to explain the meaning of the term 'stakeholder'):

- Who do you consider to be a stakeholder in this course?
- Why do you consider these people to be stakeholders?

Now ask representatives from each category of stakeholder what they consider the purposes of the course to be.

You may find it difficult to obtain directly the sort of information you are seeking from course funders, especially those associated with central government. You may need to infer it from material published by, for instance, central government funding agencies.

Use the information you have collected as the basis for a discursive paper which describes:

- the theories or models of education implied by the responses from the various stakeholders;
- the ways in which the course meets the needs of the various stakeholders with whom you have consulted;
- the potential or actual tensions that may arise because of the differing implicit theories of teaching held by the different stakeholders;
- some of the long-term consequences of the differing implicit theories of teaching held by the different stakeholders.

Developing Reflective Practice: A Case Study

A typical enquiry might be initially focused on an entire course module, or a term or semester's work with a group of students. The following example began with the study of an 11-week design and technology subsidiary subject course that was conducted as an option for BEd students in the first year of their four-year primary teacher education course.

This was a course that aimed to develop the students' problem-solving skills in a technological context. It also provided an introduction to the primary school design and technology curriculum. The students were encouraged to develop their skills of evaluation in both the problem-solving processes that they followed and in terms of the final solutions that they arrived at. Subsidiary aims included the need for the students to become increasingly aware of the range of solutions possible for the problems, to develop collaborative group work and greater skill in the use of a range of tools and workshop equipment.

The tutor provided the students with a new design problem each week and students, in groups of three or four, were required to present their solution the following week along with their notes showing the approach taken, the design problems encountered and their overall evaluation of the work.

Rather than setting progressively more demanding problems, the tutor chose to encourage self-reflection and to encourage solutions of increasing sophistication. The development of critical/evaluative skills were thus considered a very high priority. The students' 'critical and reflective logs' were returned each week with comments to provide continuous 'formative' feedback. The tasks that were set included competitive 'egg race' activities, the production of a mechanical 'cooking timer/alarm' and a child's toy. In some of the activities the students were required to design products that would satisfy the needs of people in very different economic and environmental circumstances. The toy was to be designed for a 4-year-old boy and the brief required that it should be motivating and encourage caring and non-violent play.

On completion of the course a thorough evaluation was carried out. Most of the students had made significant progress in terms of the overall aims of the course although one student was poorly motivated: 'to me it was just a component to pass for my main subject'. Two of the students felt that they had been 'thrown into the deep end' (given the difficulties they had always experienced with creative work).

While many of the students had made considerable progress in developing their creative/evaluative skills, a significant minority appeared to resist the acceptance of any definition of technology that included sociological, philosophical and affective components. This was particularly apparent in dealing with issues of 'race', 'gender' and 'appropriate technology'. The tutor felt that the students' evaluations were often too shallow and (to adopt the terms suggested by Ashcroft and Griffiths above) neither 'open-minded' nor 'responsible'.

The students reported upon their enjoyment of the course and on their improved knowledge of the subject, their learning of problem-solving strategies and skills, of time management and planning, group work and craft skills. Most of the students reported feeling much more confident in designing and making activities.

The form of the evaluation also encouraged the students to identify a number of key skills that they felt were required to successfully complete the course. Most students emphasized the need to develop 'good imagination', group working and collaborative skills as well as the development of manufacturing capability which included the use of various tools. The following skills were also considered important by some of the students:

Initiative	Practical skills
Adaptability	Modelling ideas
Sense of humour	Open-mindedness
Patience	Craft skills
Artistic	

While the students failed to identify 'problem solving', it was implicit in many of their responses. Evaluative skills were not specifically mentioned, and this was despite the strong emphasis that was placed on evaluation and the progress made by many of the students in writing their 'critically reflective' reports.

The tutor decided that he needed to make his students more aware of the processes of evaluation that they were engaged in. It was felt that there was a need to develop teaching methods that encouraged the students to identify their first assumptions and to critically engage with them. A science seminar involving a group of year-four BEd students provided an opportunity to test an initial strategy. The main object of the seminar was to show the students how they might teach their pupils about 'the Earth in space'. By this stage of the course the students had already developed a range of preferred teaching strategies and the students were initially asked (anonymously) to:

> Provide an outline plan of a lesson you would give in ideal circumstances (ie, students 100 per cent responsive, attentive and curious) to a group of students who are to be taught the spherical nature of the Earth.

The students were then directed to work in groups discussing pupil responses to an unrelated problem on energy while the tutor read through and deconstructed their lesson plans. The tutor then reported on their responses and initiated a discussion of them.

Twelve of the 15 students in the first cohort began their lesson by telling or explaining the spherical nature of the Earth to the children.
Ten suggested the use of a globe or Earth model.
Four suggested showing satellite pictures of the Earth.
Two suggested that it was important to move gradually from the child's local surroundings out to the global concept.
Three suggested the use of 'maps' at some point.
Two suggested discussing 'journeys' with the children.
Two suggested discussing day and night.

One student referred to the use of visual evidence.
One student suggested beginning by asking the children to draw a
    picture of the Earth.
One suggested 'finding out what the child knows'.

A critical discussion of some of the assumptions that were being made
about the children's prior understandings was then followed by a
presentation illustrating classroom 'constructivist' approaches to teaching 'energy', 'floating and sinking' and 'particle theory'. In each case
the suggested lessons began by identifying the children's prior knowledge and then engaging with this. Constructivist approaches to science
teaching are increasingly popular; such perspectives are based upon the
notion that we construct mental models of phenomena and that any
new experiences are interpreted and understood in those terms.

At the end of the session the students were asked to note any changes
in their plans for teaching 'the spherical nature of the Earth'. This time all
15 students suggested some form of child-centred 'constructivist' lesson:

Five suggested beginning by asking about/discussing the shape of the
    Earth.
Six suggested 'finding out what the children know' by drawing a picture
    or making a model.
Four suggested that it was necessary to begin with the child's own
    concept and build on or disprove their ideas using practical and visual
    aids as far as possible.
Three suggested the need to move from local to global.
Three suggested that the children 'investigate'.
Two suggested the use of a globe.
Two suggested using historical sources (eg, Columbus).

A second group of students responded somewhat differently: 11 of the
14 students in this group suggested some form of constructivist lesson
from the beginning. Four suggested they would begin by asking the
children to 'draw a picture'. At the end of the session, three of the 11
'constructivists' said that they wouldn't change their lessons. Others
referred to the need for more:

debate on alternative ideas (eg, flat Earth) (three)
hands-on experience (two)
use of historical sources (two)
emphasis on children's own ideas (two)
use of videos (one).

Of the three non-constructivists, two didn't change their plans. The other wrote: 'Perhaps I would ask the children what they thought first before introducing globes, etc... I would look at video and photographic evidence'.

The most significant finding was the degree of difference between the two groups. The tutor discovered that had a constructivist approach not been taken, the same lecture would have been provided to both groups quite inappropriately. This reinforced the tutor's resolve to adopt constructivist methods throughout his teaching and he adopted a similar approach in the next first-year design and technology class that he took. Each session began with brainstorming and group discussions. Each group presented one or more potential solutions and this created an environment where the students were able to benefit from the critical evaluations of others. Both the tutor's observations and the end-of-course evaluations showed that the students became much more aware of the initial assumptions that they made and were progressively more willing to adapt their plans in the light of alternative suggestions.

RESEARCH TASK. DEVELOPING STUDENTS' SELF-REFLECTION

Decide what might be indicators of reflective practice within your own subject. In particular, identify indicators of student attitudes and behaviour with respect to:

- open-mindedness;
- responsibility; and
- commitment.

Design an activity that will enable students to demonstrate these indicators of reflective attitudes and behaviours.

Get the students to undertake the activity and categorize them into groups according to their apparent attitudes and behaviour.

Check your categorization through careful questioning.

Design discussion and other activities aimed at enabling students to develop more self-reflective attitudes and behaviour.

Assess the extent to which the students have achieved the aims.

Annotated Reading List

Apple, M (1986) *Teachers and Texts: A political economy of class and gender relations in education,* London: Routledge.
This text provides a critical analysis of the managerial and conservative

trends that we have seen in educational policy and practice. The changes in educational content and control are related to changes in the social relations of class and gender.

Cornbleth, C (1990) *Curriculum in Context,* London: Falmer Press.
An influential introductory text.

Day, C, Calderhead, J and Denicolo, P (eds) (1993) *Research on Teacher Thinking: Understanding professional development,* London: Falmer Press.
Another core text, this reader provides a broad introduction to the subject of curriculum studies as it was originally conceived and instituted.

Dewey, J (1938) *Experience and Education,* New York: Collier Books.
Provides a very useful and relevant critique of educational 'isms', including progressivism. The book also provides a concise and clear statement of Dewey's educational philosophy.

Lawton, D (1992) *Education and Politics in the 1990s: Conflict or consensus?,* London: Falmer Press.
It would be useful to read this book in conjunction with Apple (1986) (above). Lawton provides an analysis of the education service that relates to recent changes in ideological differences between and within the dominant political parties in the UK.

Miller, J (1988) *The Holistic Curriculum,* Toronto: OISE Press.
A well-researched and thought-provoking text that promotes educational humanism and curriculum integration. As with many of the other texts, while the arguments are mainly applied to childhood and schooling, they may be considered equally relevant in other educational contexts.

Moon, B, Murphy, P and Raynor, J (eds) (1989) *Policies for the Curriculum,* London: Hodder and Stoughton.
A review of developments in curriculum research in the 1980s. The book documents the politicization of the curriculum and offers a number of pragmatic options for encouraging change in policy and practice.

Stenhouse, L (1975) *An Introduction to Curriculum Research and Development,* Oxford: Heinemann.
This classic curriculum studies text has been extremely influential in promoting the notion of 'teacher as researcher'. The book covers all the main issues related to the content of education, teaching behavioural objectives and curriculum development.

Taylor, P (1985) *An Introduction to Curriculum Studies,* Walton-on-Thames: NFER-Nelson.
An introductory text that provides all the basic concepts and definitions. A book to engage with.

Whitty, G (1985) *Sociology and School Knowledge: Curriculum theory, research and politics,* London: Methuen.
This book focuses on the attempts that have been made to gear schooling more closely to the needs of industry. The early chapters provide a very useful introductory review of the changing perspectives that have been taken by theorists in educational sociology and curriculum studies.

References

Ashcroft, K and Foreman-Peck, L (1994), *Managing Teaching and Learning in Further and Higher Education,* London: Falmer Press.

Ashcroft, K and Griffiths, M (1989) 'Reflective teachers and reflective tutors: school experience in an initial teacher education course', *Journal of Education for Teaching,* 15, 1, 57–70.

Apple, M (1979) *Ideology and the Curriculum,* London: Routledge and Kegan Paul.

Banister, P, Burman, E, Parker, I, Taylor, M and Tindall, C (1994) *Qualitative Methods in Psychology: A research guide,* Buckingham: Open University Press.

Becker, H and Geer, B (1982) 'Participant observation: the analysis of qualitative field data', in Burgess, R (ed.) *Field Research: A sources book and field manual,* London: George Allen and Unwin.

Brown, G and Atkins, M (1988) *Effective Teaching in Higher Education,* London: Methuen.

Carr, C (1993) 'Editorial', *Curriculum Studies,* 1, 1, 1–2.

Cohen, L and Manion, L (1994) *Research Methods in Education (4th edn),* London: Routledge.

Cormack, M (1992) *Ideology,* London: Batsford.

Derrida, J (1967) *Of Grammatology,* London: Johns Hopkins University Press.

Elliot, J (1991) 'A model of professionalism and its implications for teacher education', *British Educational Research Journal,* 17, 4, 309–18.

Foucault, M (1969) *The Archaeology of Knowledge,* London: Tavistock.

Foucault, M (1977) *Discipline and Punish: birth of the prison,* Harmondsworth: Penguin.

Giroux, H (1992) *Border Crossings: Cultural workers and the politics of education,* London: Routledge.

Goodson, I (1983) *School Subjects and Curriculum Change,* Beckenham: Croom Helm.

Grundy, S (1987) *Curriculum: Product or praxis?,* Toronto: OISE Press.

Lawton, D (1989) *Education, Culture and the National Curriculum,* London: Hodder and Stoughton.

Sarup, M (1988) *An Introductory Guide to Post-Structuralism and Postmodernism,* Hemel Hempstead: Harvester-Wheatsheaf.

Siraj-Blatchford, I (1993) 'Ethnicity and conflict in physical education: a critique of Carroll and Hollinshead's study', *British Educational Research Journal,* 19, 1, 77–82.

Tesch, R (1990) *Qualitative Research: Analysis types and software tools,* London: Falmer Press.

van Dijk, T (1985) *Handbook of Discourse Analysis, Vol. 4,* London: Academic Press.

Weiner, G (1989) 'Professional self-knowledge versus social justice: a critical analysis of the teacher-researcher movement', *British Educational Research Journal,* 15, 1, 41–2.

Winter, R (1991) 'Postmodern sociology as a democratic educational practice? Some suggestions', *British Journal of Sociology of Education,* 12, 4, 467–82.

Woods, P (1979) *The Divided School,* London: Routledge and Kegan Paul.

Young, M (ed.) (1970) *Knowledge and Control,* Buckingham: Open University Press.

Chapter 6

Micro-politics, Participation and Empowerment

Power Relations in Colleges and Universities

There can be little doubt that differential power relations exist in our colleges and universities. Much research has been conducted to demonstrate the existence of these differentials and it has often documented the struggles of particular groups in gaining equality of participation. We might also consider the case of Laurie Taylor's regular weekly column in the *Times Higher Educational Supplement*. Because we share a common understanding of the power relations which exist in (and between) colleges and universities, we can share these humorous episodes each week which are based on the fictitious goings-on at the University of Poppleton. In this column, Taylor often draws particular attention to the differential power relations of principals and vice-chancellors, of academic staff, and their long-suffering secretarial staff and students. The current contexts and stresses within higher education, examination boards, research assessment exercises and the pressures to publish refereed papers for example, are all satirized through the interactions of the regular caricatures. We laugh because we share a common understanding of the underpinning assumptions and relations, and because these are often ridiculed or exaggerated to an extreme.

Students are also acutely aware of the 'system' within which they operate. Many student course evaluations reveal their concerns and anxieties about everyday issues such as lectures and assessments. Students often complain if the tutor who set their assignment does not first-mark it: in such cases they may consider themselves at a disadvantage. This implies that they are writing for particular tutors, whom they perceive as fairly subjective, and at least powerful enough to assert their interpretation of a 'good' piece of work. It is not unusual for students to complain when other students make seminar presentations, which they perceive as not allowing the tutor enough time to impart his or her specialist knowledge. From these examples, which many of us will recognize, it seems that students often collude with the system and many remain compliant in the face of differential power relations. They may seek to challenge their individual tutor but they rarely engage with the system as a whole. The reasons for this are complex, but clearly any challenge to the status quo is both extremely threatening and time-consuming. Students only have a few years (or less) of study at any particular institution. Tutors are in a far better position to influence change.

RESEARCH ACTIVITY. AN IDEOLOGICAL DECONSTRUCTION OF STUDENT EVALUATIONS

Take a sample of students' written course evaluations.

- Conduct an ideological analysis to ascertain some of their assumptions and assertions about the course as a whole and their expectations of tutors and of themselves in the process of teaching and learning.
- Devise a coding schedule which reveals the most common experiences that students have on the course and those aspects which they refer to in particular ways.

Try doing this for each of your courses. Are there any patterns which emerge?

The most significant power differentials in colleges and universities may be identified in a number of contexts:

- power ascribed through patriarchal and gendered relations;
- racialized hierarchies within institutions;
- hierarchies related to socio-economic class;
- differential treatment of older and younger people;
- relationships between academic staff and students;
- relationships between academic staff, ancillary/administrative staff and students;
- lack of recognition of differences between non-traditional and traditional student support;
- the power relations within academic teaching groups, departments, faculty and research teams.

Each of these contexts is interrelated and the power differentials within any of the groups mentioned above may be as great as those between the groups. This chapter is concerned mainly with the differential power relations between academic staff and students; however, some of the other categories mentioned above will overlap with this. Some very capable studies focused on the power struggles between teaching staff and departments have been carried out (Paechter, 1993). The categories are listed simply to show the range of differences and issues which might exist and interrelate.

The inequalities of status and power in our colleges and universities are taken for granted by most staff and students on a routine basis: they are considered as part of the natural order of things. But they also provide a very interesting topic for research and publication. Very few of us actually feel powerful enough to challenge these differentials in our daily practice and yet research offers the prospect of a form of 'academic distance'. It may be that the more powerful we become the less temptation there is to share our power, but as we shall see it might often be wise to consider the practical as well as the moral benefits to be gained from doing so.

RESEARCH ACTIVITY. STRATIFICATION SURVEY

Conduct a statistical audit of the staff and students in your institution by gender, ethnic background, age, status and position.

If you are in a position to do so, also conduct an audit using the same categories with regard to cleaning, secretarial, library, administrative and catering staff.

Are there any patterns that emerge?

How does this relate to policy, practice and the monitoring and action taken by your department and institution in terms of equality of opportunity?

Micro-politics

Micro-politics is about power and how people use it to influence others and to protect themselves. It is about conflict and how people compete with each other to get what they want. It is about co-operation and how people build support among themselves to achieve their ends. It is about what people in all social settings think about and have strong feelings about, but what is so often unspoken and not easily observed. The micro-political perspective presents practising administrators and scholars alike with fresh and provocative ways to think about human behaviour in schools (Blase, 1991, p.1).

In his introduction to micro-politics as an analytic tool, Ball (1987) contrasts its assumptions with those of a more traditional organizational science perspective. Ball presents what he sees as the major distinctions between the two perspectives in the list of 'key concepts' in Table 6.1.

Table 6.1 *Micro-political and organizational science perspectives (reproduced from Ball, 1987, p.8)*

Micro-political perspective	Organizational science perspective
Power	Authority
Goal diversity	Goal coherence
Ideological disputation	Ideological neutrality
Conflict	Consensus
Interests	Motivation
Political activity	Decision-making
Control	Consent

Ball argues that the organizational science perspective often paints a model of an institution as it would wish to be seen; its public face, rather than its more messy and fractured reality. Power relations are seen unproblematically as relations of authority. As Blase (1991, p.3) suggests:

In essence, political theorists have argued that rational and systems models of organizations have failed to account for complexity, instability and conflict in organizational settings. They contend that such models also ignore individual differences, for example, in values, ideologies, choices, goals, interests, expertise, history, motivation, and interpretation – factors central to the micro-political perspective.

There is in fact no single micro-political perspective. The key concepts identified in Table 6.1 may be articulated in a variety of ways. Ball's own analysis is limited to just three 'key and interrelated areas of organizational activity':

- the interests of actors;
- the maintenance of organizational control;
- conflict over policy.

Any combination, or all of the key concepts may thus be relevant to your own research context.

Power

A micro-political approach would provide a focus on the organizational culture and upon the way that power operates often in unofficial and unintended ways. The micro-political processes may also be linked to macro-political pressures.

Goal diversity

In education, we certainly cannot assume a consensus regarding goals. Individual lecturers and tutors typically have goals determined by a complex set of experiences, including their own educational experience, their training, their political affiliations and their socialization into their subject sub-cultures.

Ideology

Many of the decisions taken in colleges and universities are of necessity value-laden; education is often ideological by design. Lecturers and tutors will have differing views on equality of opportunity and academic justice that will fundamentally inform their decisions.

Conflict

The recognition of conflict is fundamental to micro-political analysis. Ball (1987) cites Baldridge (1971) in identifying the main tenets of the conflict perspective that are applied in his study:

1. Conflict theorists emphasise the fragmentation of social systems into interest groups, each with its own particular goals.
2. Conflict theorists study the interaction of these different interest groups and especially the conflict processes by which one group tries to gain advantage over another.
3. Interest groups cluster around divergent values, and the study of conflicting interests is a key part of the analysis.
4. The study of change is a central feature of the conflict approach, for change is to be expected if the social system is fragmented by divergent values and conflicting interest groups (p.18)

Interests

Ball discusses three types of interests held by teachers and these might just as easily be applied to lecturers and tutors: vested interests, ideological interests and self-interests. The vested interests arise from the differential access to, and control of, resources as well as those other material concerns of individuals and groups such as salaries, working conditions and career development. Ideological interests such as values and philosophical commitments provide another source of contention. As Ball suggests, these interests often involve individuals and groups in relating practical issues to more fundamental political or philosophical positions. The term 'self-interest' is used here to refer to the self-identity held by individuals and groups. Some lecturers and tutors may see themselves in differing degrees as teachers, administrators and research academics and scholars.

Political activity

While it would be foolish to assume that all decisions are politically motivated, it would clearly be equally foolish to assume that all decisions are made by individuals and groups without reference to the pursuit of a strategic advantage. A micro-political approach draws the researcher's attention to the specific situation that is being studied:

> the issues and the specific inclinations of individual actors. Some people may be politically active in the organisation on a regular basis; others may get involved when particular issues arise; others still never dabble in this sort of pursuit. (Ball, 1987, p.21)

Control

Three types of organizational control are commonly identified in micro-political studies: hierarchical, membership controlled, and professional communities. Teaching is usually considered a profession (Collins, 1975) yet as Ball argues, most schools (and arguably most colleges and universities) contain elements of all three forms of control. Different participants may also have very different views of both the ideal and actual form of control observed.

RESEARCH TASK. MICRO-POLITICAL ANALYSIS

- Identify some source of dispute within your institution; it may be between different faculties or departments, or it may be between different groups.
- Referring to the discussion above, note the relevance of each of the key concepts listed.

Which provides the greatest insight into the nature of the dispute?

- Make a list of all the alternative explanations of the dispute that you can think of.
- Make a list of the data you would require to confirm or refute these hypotheses.

What data collection techniques might be employed?
Conduct a small-scale research study to explore at least one of your hypotheses.

Effective Teaching and Student Participation

Feldman (1976) identified a number of characteristics associated with effective teaching in colleges and universities:

- the stimulation of interest;
- the application of clarity and good judgement;
- a good knowledge of the subject matter;
- preparation for, and organization of, the course;
- enthusiasm for both the subject matter and for teaching.

Yet, according to Perry (1970), most students enter college at a stage of intellectual development where knowledge acquisition is simply seen it terms of accumulating information. Thus it appears that students in-itially believe that their lecturer has all of the knowledge that they require and that their task is to assimilate it directly. This approach to learning has been referred to as a 'surface approach' and may be contrasted with 'deep approaches' of students who are self-motivated (see Ashcroft and Foreman-Peck, 1994, or Bennett *et al.*, 1996, for more detail on ways to enquire into students' approaches to learning). It may well be that within our educational system it is only a minority of students who ultimately reach the stage where they assume personal responsibil-ity for their own active construction and reconstruction of knowledge.

This process may be seen in terms of power acquisition. As students advance through the system they are increasingly accepted as members of an academic elite, as knowledge producers as well as knowledge accumulators. This has important implications for teaching and learning.

A recent study by Andrews *et al.* (1996) examined the relationship between students' learning approaches and their tutor's approaches to teaching. The project was developed to investigate teaching excellence in higher education as the authors argued that:

> Excellent teaching is appreciating the nature of a quality learning outcome (ie, students' understanding), and ensuring that teaching approaches and activities are congruent with achieving this outcome. (p.82)

There is evidence to suggest that both excessive workloads and an emphasis on assessment through recall are likely to encourage students to adopt surface approaches (Ramsden, 1992). While there may be limited contexts where a surface approach might be of value – in the acquisition of narrow technical skills and competences for example – for the mass of students we are likely to prioritize meaningful and integrated learning. As Andrews *et al.* (1996, p.84) suggest:

> encouraging students to make decisions and providing opportunities to analyse and synthesise information in a respectful environment is an approach to teaching that must be considered.

They argue that the improvement of teaching can only be achieved through addressing the basic beliefs and values of teachers. The contradictions between their espoused theories and their practices need to be made apparent to them. Teachers' beliefs and values also need to be evaluated in the light of their students approaches to learning. Their study, which we summarize below, was conducted in four phases.

Case Study: The Teaching and Learning Transaction

Below we outline a study of excellent professors and their students from the University of Calgary in Canada.

Phase 1

In phase 1 of the study, an initial profile of excellence in university teaching was developed from extended interviews with education faculty members. The interviews were structured around five themes: the intended outcomes; the teaching and learning processes used to attain the outcomes; the values, beliefs and characteristics of the lecturers; the barriers to role performance; and the specific instructional strategies that supported the teaching and learning processes:

> common themes were identified by the research team using a constant comparison method. The themes under each of the five categories were then assembled into a 'profile' and presented to the faculty members for validation. (Andrews *et al.*, 1996, p.84)

Six areas of excellence were finally identified in the profile:

1. *Overview*. Teaching excellence was considered to be based on three related factors:

   - valuing students;
   - valuing the subject matter; and
   - valuing the process of teaching.

2. *Outcomes*. It was considered that students should be able to transfer their classroom learning to 'real life' and it was felt that the transfer of learning involved the development of self-reflective and self-directed students.

3. *Processes*. Processes should reflect the need to make content meaningful and relevant to students. These needs were described in terms of three major areas:

   - the ongoing commitment of the lecturer to self-reflection, collaboration with colleagues and thorough preparation and organization;
   - strong and respectful relationship between the lecturer and their students; collaboration in the learning process was seen as important;
   - the encouragement of independent thought through discussion and other interactive strategies and the use of formative methods of evaluation.

4. *Values, beliefs and characteristics*. Teaching methods based on honesty, integrity and genuineness were seen to precipitate the self-reflective processes. The lecturer should believe that respect – for themselves, for the material and for the processes of teaching – provides an essential foundation to effective practice.

5. *Barriers*. The main barriers to effective teaching that were identified

related to:

- over-work;
- administrative responsibilities;
- misdirected 'accountability'; and
- incapable colleagues.

6. *Specific knowledge/skills.* The need for basic communication and interactive skills was emphasized as well as the possession of a range of teaching strategies to accommodate a variety of instructional settings.

Phase 2

In the second phase of the study, the social science and science faculty members were asked to identify two specific lecturers who taught different (year one and year three) groups and who both exhibited excellence in their teaching. These lecturers were then interviewed to compare the profiles across departments and year groups.

The interview data showed that there was a strong similarity between all of the four teaching profiles from all three faculties. The lecturers shared common understandings of what constituted excellence. There were differences however, in the responses of lecturers in the context of 'barriers' and in terms of the specific instructional strategies and skills. The year-one lecturers particularly noted the quantity of subject matter to be covered and discussed their use of multiple-choice examinations. The year-three lecturers made no references to course content as a barrier, nor to multiple-choice examinations. The year-three tutors adopted more open-ended assignments for assessment.

Phase 3

In the third phase of the study a questionnaire was completed by the two first-year classes and two third-year classes of the lecturers interviewed in phase 2. The Study Process Questionnaire (SPQ) developed in Australia by Biggs (1982) was used, and the students assessed as either 'surface', 'deep' or 'achieving' learners. The surface and deep categories have already been discussed; for the purposes of the study, 'achieving' learners were considered to be those who adopted highly systematic study strategies and those motivated predominantly by the achievement of high grades. Andrews *et al.* (1996) provide a useful summary of Biggs' theory and this is reproduced here in Table 6.2.

Table 6.2 *Biggs' approaches to learning and corresponding motives and strategies*

Approach	Motive	Strategies
Surface	Extrinsic; avoid failure, but don't work too hard; learning in school is a means towards some other end getting a job	Focus on selected details and reproduce; learn by rote memorization
Deep	Intrinsic; satisfy curiosity about topic, sees learning task as interesting and personally involving, wants to develop special interests and abilities	Maximize understanding, focus on meaning rather than on literal aspects, read widely, discuss, reflect, integrate and elaborate information
Achieving	Achievement; ego-enhancement, obtain high stature, maximize grades	Optimize organization of time and effort; use of study skills (ie planning, reviewing, following course outlines, etc)

Phase 4

In the final phase of the study a sub-sample of 20 students was drawn from the first- and the third-year classes. They were then interviewed to gain further knowledge of their approach to learning and their perceptions of their lecturers' approach to teaching.

The study findings

While no significant differences were found in the approaches of lecturers, the students clearly differed in their responses to the SPQ. The lecturers all favoured deep approaches to learning yet the first-year students were predominantly inclined towards surface approaches; it was only the third-year students who tended to adopt a deep approach. An incongruence between the first-year lecturers' approach to teaching and their students' approach to learning was therefore identified. The interviews revealed that the first-year students tended to be preoccupied with achievement and grades while more of the third years expressed an intrinsic interest in their subject. The authors suggest lecturers might be advised to limit the scope of the curriculum, especially in the early years of the students' course. This would provide the students with more time to 'think, understand the major concepts, broaden their frame of reference, and to construct frameworks for meaningful learning'. As Andrews *et al.* clearly identify, the study also has implications for higher education in general:

> If the primary outcome is for students to be independent learners and to construct knowledge that is personally meaningful and valid, then it will be necessary for students to assume considerable responsibility for constructing meaning and to participate collaboratively in educational decisions. The challenge is for professors [lecturers] to develop higher cognitive abilities and move away from prescriptive packaging of content. (1996, p.98)

However, this kind of student 'empowerment' has a number of other implications that should be carefully considered before embarking upon any radical programme.

RESEARCH TASK. EMERGING DATA CATEGORIES

The emergence of data categories may be considered more of a phenomenon than a technique or methodology as such. It is, however, an area about which many of those approaching research for the first time are especially concerned.

In the early stages of a research project it is often very difficult to imagine the form that the analysis will take. This is probably a good thing, as any kind of prescription is likely to introduce bias, but this is unlikely to be much consolation for those anxious that all their data collection efforts might eventually be wasted. All we can offer to those readers with similar fears is encouragement to accept that all research projects by their very nature involve this kind of leap into the unknown. The worry that you may initially feel is a natural response and it is something that you are likely put behind you as you gain more confidence and experience. Throughout the book we have suggested a number of illustrations of the kind of analytical processes you might employ to encourage your data categories to 'emerge'; this task is offered as an exercise that might give you more confidence with your own project.

Ask each of your colleagues to spend just a few minutes writing a short description of the sort of circumstances and events that constitute for them an ideal example of 'good practice' in teaching.

Look through each of the responses and make a note of all of those characteristics that appear in more than one response. These are your first categories and you will probably find that they 'emerge' quite easily.

Give each of these categories a number code and see if you can draw some of them together into clusters of related groups. You may find that you need to cut up the pieces of paper to do this; if so, you will need to put your respondents' names on each fragment of their response. An alternative is to duplicate the responses or to use a computer. However the task is approached, these new groups will provide higher order categories.

Draw a schematic diagram showing the structure of your categorization. On your diagram try to show how the different categories may be related to each other.

At this stage you will be beginning to form explanatory models or theories that can be tested through further data collection.

For a more elaborate exercise you might first construct a semi-structured interview schedule using four of Andrews *et al.*'s five themes, noting:

- the intended teaching outcomes;
- the processes used to attain the outcomes;
- the values, beliefs and characteristics of your colleagues; and
- the specific instructional strategies that supported the processes.

You may also wish to obtain a copy of Biggs' SPQ and take the study even further to discover how these perceptions match with those of their students.

At the end of this chapter our reading list includes Day *et al.* (1993). This book elaborates upon what Pope (1993), in her significant contributory chapter to the edited collection, refers to as the pre-paradigmatic field of research into teacher thinking. The book is concerned with school teacher thinking, yet many of the insights that it provides are valuable at any level of practice. Pope suggests that professional researchers should ask themselves whether they research from the 'outside in' or the 'inside out' and whether they really 'accept and respect teachers' experienced knowledge'. In the light of Andrews *et al.*'s research, perhaps we should be looking beyond these concerns to ask ourselves similar questions regarding the 'experienced knowledge' of our students.

Student Empowerment and 'Critical Pedagogy'

The popularity of notions of student 'empowerment' in colleges and universities undoubtedly stems from the widespread acceptance that many students in the past and at present have been actively disempowered by education. Most of us have felt, at some point in our academic experience, that we have been 'put down' by someone who has expert knowledge in some field or other. Cultural stereotyping is such that some groups are more vulnerable to being 'put down' in some subjects than others. Women are thus often disadvantaged in information technology classes. Working-class and ethnic minority students are also vulnerable and there is always the danger that students begin to identify themselves according to the prejudiced perceptions of others. Students may lose confidence and this may in turn lead to underachievement or even failure.

Ethnic majority, middle-class and male lecturers may thus be particularly concerned to ensure that they do not unwittingly disempower their students. In an increasingly post-modern environment, many lecturers will also be concerned to show that they understand that all of their 'knowing' is partial. They may well wish to emphasize that there is no ultimate authority in the seminar or lecture theatre. Whatever their degree of commitment to empowerment, lecturers in this situation will wish to encourage their students to find their own voices, to 'talk back' as Hooks (1989) has put it.

In committing themselves to the promotion of an equal dialogue lecturers are often faced with some difficult decisions; for instance, when students choose to remain silent should this be taken as subordination or as a refusal to engage with the subject under discussion. You might look at whether the seminar room should be considered as some form of idealized public sphere (a locus of citizenship) that depends upon mutual trust, sharing, respect and freedom (Giroux, 1992), or whether we should accept that decisions might often need to be made according to the lowest possible common denominator of agreement (Ellsworth, 1989). If we are dealing with sensitive subjects that are associated with equality of opportunity and human rights it may often be quite difficult for individuals with differing experiences and even more crucially those enjoying different privileges, to discuss issues without at least appearing to put each other down:

> Our classroom was not in fact a safe space for students to speak out or talk back about their experiences of oppression both inside and outside of the classroom. In our class, these included experiences

of being gay, lesbian, fat, women of color working with men of color, White women working with men of color, men of color working with White women and men. Things were not being said for a number of reasons. These included fear of being misunderstood and/or disclosing too much and becoming too vulnerable; memories of bad experiences in other contexts of speaking out; resentment that other oppressions (sexism, heterosexism, fat oppression, classism, anti-Semitism) were being marginalized in the name of addressing racism – and guilt for feeling such resentment; confusion about levels of trust and commitment surrounding those who were allies to another group's struggles; resentment by some students of color for feeling that they were expected to disclose 'more' and once again take the burden of doing the pedagogic work of educating White students/professor about the consequences of White middle-class privilege; and resentment by White students for feeling that they had to prove they were not the enemy. (Ellsworth, 1989, p.316)

In these circumstances, Ellsworth chose to develop a learning environment based on a coalition rather than a collective. She felt that the friendships that some members of her diverse media studies group had formed provided a strong basis for development. This meant accepting that the group would be defined in terms of differences rather than secure commonalities. Unity was achieved through accepting that each student had different strengths and that each provided different 'forces for change'. Ellsworth supported her different 'affinity groups' in the realization of common projects, and they supported each other in bringing proposals forward to the whole class to see how each group's plans might effect the others and also to create collaboration and broader support.

Such an example demonstrates the ultimate difficulties that student empowerment may entail. Our own feeling is that in a good many cases the broader democratic ends may justify similarly contradictory means. It should be recognized that in higher education many of our educational environments display comparatively little diversity. Often the students that we teach are drawn from the most privileged groups in society. In such cases 'empowerment' may be even more problematic and difficult to justify. It may often be the case that these students need to be confronted with alternative and oppositional voices instead.

Reflection or Refraction?

As previously argued, both reflective practice and action research involve the comparison of the lecturer's teaching and learning plans against practical reality. Students will inevitably be unable to accommodate or assimilate fully some of the 'plans' that are presented to them.

The same concept of reflection that is assumed in the reflective practitioner paradigm has been criticized, most notably by Rorty (1980). While the substance of Rorty's arguments are beyond the scope of this text, the post-modern implications are that we should now drop the subjective – objective distinction or dichotomy altogether, as well as any *scientific* conception of truth that is based on the assumed capability of theories to either directly correspond to reality or at least progressively provide better approximations of it. Such post-modern arguments are gaining considerable ground in educational research and may ultimately become the dominant paradigm. The ideals of an 'unforced agreement' for objectivity and an 'open-minded exploration' for subjectivity will then be substituted. 'Agreement' and 'exploration' will be seen as different modes of thought, related procedurally in our ongoing lifelong experience and re-experience of the natural and social world. One of the implications of these philosophical approaches suggests that the *only* legitimate forms of knowledge creation might ultimately resemble action research and critical reflection.

Our discussion of constructivism in Chapter 5 drew attention to our students' preconceived ideas and schemas, and clearly the passive concept of reflection and the mind as a mirror of reality is inherently conservative and allows no possibility for any kind of paradigm shift. To return to our earlier discussion, while reflection may be committed, it may be neither open-minded nor responsible. Our aims in education are quite often to provide students with another way of looking, an appreciation of alternative perspectives and paradigms. If we are to confront inequality then it is clear that we require educational and research models that recognize what Kelly (1955) termed the 'spectacles' through which we perceive reality. If we are to address value issues we need to provide students with alternative 'spectacles'. Spectacle lenses distort images through refraction and the principle of refractive teaching may therefore provide a more adequate basis for continued development.

In practice this would mean being more prescriptive at times, providing the clear plans to test in practice with our students, and to collaboratively 'refract upon'. It would also involve a more consistent and self-conscious attempt at developing students' explicit understandings of the learning models that are being applied. Constructivist approaches offer a possible means for such development and for lecturers in initial teacher education at least, the adoption of such methods will represent no more than practising more effectively what they already preach. These very same principles also need to be applied, reflexively, to our own research practices so that we accept that as lecturers researching our own practices, we have no privileged perspective to be applied. We should have no illusions regarding the status of our own values, beliefs and perceptions.

The structure and style of the research that we are proposing is thus based upon a radical philosophical approach that provides no episte-mological grounding but rather a continued refraction on the process of enquiry. Such refractions could be into the nature of things (ie, scientific) or into the shaping of things (technology). We may be predominantly concerned to develop a greater knowledge and under-standing of the teaching and learning process or we may be more concerned to develop our practice (or 'praxis'; see Siraj-Blatchford, 1994).

In Chapter 5, Winter (1991) was cited as arguing that education is inevitably 'always both theoretical practice and practical theory'. A useful insight is provided by Huberman (1993) who tackles the theory-practice problem from a perspective that emphasizes the significance of our 'dissemination and utilisation of knowledge'. Huberman pro-vides a particularly valuable and stimulating account of research based upon what he describes as a 'sustained interactivity' between the re-searcher and the researched. While the model assumes a clear separa-tion of role between researchers and their respondents, a number of important issues are clarified.

There can be little doubt that, as Huberman suggests, many main-stream researchers in education have, in the past, seen dissemination as something of a distraction from their priorities. This has important implications. The elaboration of a sustained 'dialogic' (Harvey, 1990) between researchers and respondents probably offers us the greatest challenge and opportunities for the future development of good prac-tice. As stated earlier, your choice of research methodology will be determined by the personal aims that you have for your research. If your central concern is to inform your practice directly then you probably have little to fear from embarking upon a collaborative investigation with your students. If, by contrast, you wish to contribute towards the development of some form of academic knowledge base on teaching and learning, you will wish to adopt a more traditional approach, trying to avoid any 'contamination' of your data.

Whichever approach is adopted there are many publication possibilities open to you and it is to this subject that we turn in the final chapter.

Annotated Reading List

Day, C, Calderhead, J and Denicolo, P (eds) (1993) *Research on Teacher Thinking: Understanding professional development*, London, Falmer Press.
A collection of studies in an area that may be considered to offer a new paradigm in curriculum studies 'teacher thinking'.

Polity Press (1994) *The Polity Reader in Gender Studies*, Cambridge: Polity Press in Association with Blackwell.
The title says it all – these are essential readings.

Shor, I (1992) *Empowering Education*, Chicago, Ill: University of Chicago Press.
An analysis of the opportunities and limitations of empowerment in education. Examples are drawn from both school and higher/adult educational contexts.

Skeggs, B (1991) 'Postmodernism: what is all the fuss about?', *British Journal of Sociology of Education*, 12, 2, 255–7.
A valuable review essay covering four influential edited collections on postmodernism, all published between 1988 and 1990.

Young, M (1993) 'A curriculum for the 21st century? Towards a new bias for overcoming academic/vocational divisions', *British Journal of Educational Studies*, 4, 4, 203–22.
Young argues that changes in the organization of labour and the economy provide an opportunity for overcoming the academic and vocational divisions that have dominated post-compulsory education.

References

Andrews, J, Garrison, D and Magnusson, K (1996) 'The teaching and learning transaction in higher education: a study of excellent professors and their students', *Teaching in Higher Education*, 1, 1, March.

Ashcroft, K and Foreman-Peck, L (1994) *Managing Teaching and Learning in Further and Higher Education*, London: Falmer Press.

Baldridge, V (1971) *Power and Conflict in the University*, New York: John Wiley.

Ball, S (1987) *The Micro-politics of the School: Towards a theory of school organisation*, London: Methuen.

Bennett, C, Higgins, C and Foreman-Peck, L (1996) *Researching into Teaching Methods in Colleges and Universities*, London: Kogan Page.

Biggs, J (1982) 'Student motivation and study strategies in university and CAE populations', *Higher Education Research and Development*, 1, 33–5.

Blase, J (ed.) (1991) *The Politics of Life in Schools: Power, conflict and cooperation*, Beverley Hills, CA: Sage.

Collins, R (1975) *Conflict Sociology*, New York: Academic Press.

Ellsworth, E (1989) 'Why doesn't this feel empowering? Working through the repressive myths of critical pedagogy', *Harvard Educational Review*, 59, 3, 297–324.

Feldman, K (1976) 'The superior college teacher from the students' view', *Research in Higher Education*, 5, 243–88.

Giroux, H (1992) *Border Crossings: Cultural workers and the politics of education*, London: Routledge.

Harvey, L (1990) *Critical Social Research*, London: Unwin Hyman.

Hooks, B (1989) *Talking Back: Thinking feminist – thinking black*, London: Sheba.

Huberman, M (1993) 'Changing minds: the dissemination of research and its effects on practice and theory', in Day, C, Calderhead, J and Denicolo, P (eds) *Research on Teacher Thinking: Understanding professional development*, London: Falmer Press.

Kelly, G (1955) *The Psychology of Personal Constructs*, New York: Norton.

Paechter, C (1993) 'Power, knowledge and the design and technology curriculum', *unpublished PhD thesis*, London: Kings College.

Perry, W (1970) *Forms of Intellectual and Ethical Development in the College Years*, New York: Holt, Rinehart and Winston.

Pope, M (1993) 'Anticipating teacher thinking', in Day, C, Calderhead, J and Denicolo, P (eds) *Research on Teacher Thinking: Understanding professional development*, London: Falmer Press.

Ramsden, P (1992) *Learning to Teach in Higher Education*, London: Routledge.

Rorty, R (1980) *Philosophy and the Mirror of Nature*, Oxford: Blackwell.

Siraj-Blatchford, I (1994) *Praxis Makes Perfect: Critical educational research for social justice*, Nottingham: Education Now.

Winter, R (1991) 'Postmodern sociology as a democratic educational practice? Some suggestions', *British Journal of Sociology of Education*, 12, 4, 467–82.

Chapter 7

Series Conclusion: Getting Published

Kate Ashcroft

In this chapter I look at the process of getting published from the publisher's point of view. I outline some of the factors you might consider in choosing a publisher before going on to the describe the processes of acceptance, contract and marketing. I then look at issues particular to writing for a journal and discuss the appropriate 'voice' for different types of audience.

Most of this chapter is common to all the books in the series. If you have already read another of the *Practical Research Series,* you may want to skip the most of the following sections and go straight to the annotated list of education journals, where there will be some journals described that are particular to the topic of this book.

Books from the Publisher's Point of View

Getting started on writing a book is often the hardest part of the process. You need to convince yourself that the things that you know about and that interest you will matter sufficiently to other people to make publication worthwhile, and then you have to get down to it. You may find it reassuring to consider the small scale of much educational publishing. Modern technology has radically reduced the costs of producing a book. The economies of scale on sales beyond about 2,000 books are not particularly great, so your publisher will be pleased if you become a 'best seller' in academic book terms (sales of about 8,000 books upwards), but will not be disappointed by much more modest sales.

Once you have decided that authorship is for you, you will need to decide a focus for your book or paper. You are likely to have more success if your book is concerned with a current topic, a controversial issue or helps the reader to solve problems. Thus, books or papers that deal with new aspects of a subject (for instance, the ways that financial problems faced by university students affect their learning), with problems that people face in the course of their work or study (such as dealing with students who lack basic mathematical skills), or with a changing situation for which the readers have not been trained (for instance, helping students cope with the death of a classmate), are most likely to be welcomed by publishers or editors of journals.

In choosing a topic for a book, there is always a balance to be struck between your needs and those of the reader. For example, you may have completed a research degree on the development of essay-writing skills in students specializing in mathematics and found the subject of your dissertation interesting. However, it is likely to require a complete rewrite and reorientation of the way you approach the subject, before it becomes interesting to a larger group of readers.

Publishers receive much unsolicited material through the mail, often in the form of a covering letter and some 'finished' material. Most will consider such approaches carefully. Even so, this is likely to be the least productive way of approaching a publisher. The highest 'hit' rate is likely to be achieved if you are invited to put a proposal forward. Such invitations rarely happen by accident. They often result from putting yourself in the right place at the right time. To do this, you may need to develop networks of contacts. Commissioning editors get to know about potential authors through a number of routes. They attend conferences: you can meet them there and talk to them about your specialist area. They ask influential groups and individuals about likely authors when they perceive a niche in the market: you might get to know the committee members of relevant associations and make sure they know about your potential contribution. They often ask established writers to contribute to book series. These 'names' often already have sufficient commissions. If you can get to know established authors, and ensure that they know about you and your interests, they may suggest your name to the editor instead. Commissioning editors also read the educational press, not so much learned journals as papers such as *The Times Educational Supplement, The Times Higher Educational Supplement* and *Education.* If you have written for such papers, your name may become known in the right circles.

Editors also look for pockets of good practice and investigate them for potential authors. If your institution has had an excellent inspection report, or if you are a member of a consortium of colleges or universities that share good practice, you do not have to wait to be discovered. It may be worth drawing an editor's attention to what you are doing and to invite them to talk to you and others about its publishing potential.

I have to admit to never having acted in the ways described above. I received commissions the hard way: by putting a good quality submission to an appropriate publisher. I have been successful when I looked at the process from the editor's point of view. The publisher is much more interested in their readers' needs, and in making a profit, than in your interests. If you can present what you want to do in these terms, you may be successful. This is likely to require some research to find out who your readers are likely to be, how many of them there are, where they will be found, what their interests are and why they will want to buy your particular book.

The publisher will also be interested in the competition for the book you are proposing. If you tell him or her that there is no competition, you are likely to be asked to do more research. If you still cannot find books on your subject, the publisher may worry that there is a good reason why nobody else is publishing in that area. You may be more successful if you undertake a thorough trawl of other publications on topics related to the one that you wish to write about, and then think clearly about your particular selling points and how you can make your book better than the others on the market. Your arguments may vary, depending on what you are writing about. When I co-edited a book on the new National Curriculum, we sold it on the fact that it would be particularly timely (it was be the first book after the new Orders were published). When I wrote a book on quality and standards, I made sure that it looked at quality issues from the lecturer's point of view (others mainly wrote for institutional managers). In the case of the present series, while there are many books about insider research, and others about aspects of teaching and learning in colleges and universities, there are few that link clear and readable summaries of the current issues, for instance student support, with actual starting points for research in post-compulsory education.

Choosing a Publisher

Once you are clear about what you intend to write and who you are writing for, you will need to choose a publisher. In the UK, there are a relatively small number of publishing houses that specialize in books about education and that are interested in publishing material about further and higher education in particular. Most of the main ones feature in the list of publishers towards the end of this chapter. In addition, there are a number of publishers who are based in other countries and some universities have developed their own small in-house publishing companies.

A few academic authors use a literary agent. If you wish to do so, the *Writers' and Artists' Yearbook* will help you locate an appropriate one. The agent will place your book with an appropriate publisher, do most of the negotiation on your behalf, act as a critical friend, take care of the bookkeeping, correspondence and so on. The academic book market works with low profit margins. For this reason royalty schemes are fairly inflexible. Once you have paid his or her fees, using a literary agent is unlikely to mean that you make much more money.

If you decide to go it alone, you may find it useful to look around at the booklists of various publishers to find those that have a sizeable list in your subject. It is easier to market a group of books with a common theme. If a publisher is advertising a book series in the area of student support in tertiary education, they may be more likely to look seriously at your proposal. The next stage is to look at publishers' house-styles: the appearance of the books, the type of print and lay out, and the usual length and format of the books they produce. You will also have to decide whether to go for a large publishing house or a smaller, more specialized one. Larger houses have the marketing facilities to promote books across the world. On the other hand, junior editors in large houses have little power and may take some time to get approval for action. Small publishing houses may give more personal service. They also tend to be more highly specialized and so know a lot about publishing in a particular field.

Once you have narrowed your options, it may be useful to ask colleagues, booksellers and librarians about the reputation and effi-ciency of those publishing houses that remain on your list, before making an approach to one or more publisher. If you are new to writing for publication, it is probably worth telephoning likely publishing houses to talk to the commissioning editor for post-compulsory educa-tion or making contact with publishing representatives at conferences. You can then talk about your ideas to see if he or she is interested in them. Generally, the commissioning editor will be happy to provide you with guidelines on how to submit a formal proposal. Provided you let them know you are doing so, publishers generally do not object if you submit your book outline to two or three houses.

Once you have found a publisher you feel you can do business with, you may decide to meet. Publishing seems to be a business that thrives on personal relationships. If you deal with a publisher by letter, you may build a relationship quicker if you use their name, rather than 'sir' or 'madam'.

If the commissioning editor likes your proposal, he or she will usually ask for reports from a couple of referees. The referees' reports often contain suggestions for change. Try not be discouraged by this. It is not at all unusual to be asked for clarification, more information or slight changes before a proposal is accepted. This process can improve the proposal considerably. When I first put forward the proposal for this book series it included many more shorter books. My editor made several suggestions and I reworked the series proposals twice before we were both convinced that it was as sound as it could be.

Negotiating the Contract

Once it looks like you are more or less 'in business', you will need to discuss terms and conditions. The level of royalties offered by academic publishers does not vary greatly, but it is always worth trying to negotiate a slightly better deal or asking for a small advance on royalties, especially if you are involved in some immediate expenses (for instance, a new computer or photographic material). Whatever terms you eventually agree, it is important to read your contract carefully. Most are fairly standard. You may be paid royalties as a percentage of the net price. On the other hand, especially if your book is of the type that may be sold at a discount (for instance, through book clubs), your royalties may be a percentage of net receipts (what the publishing house actually receives from sales). This arrangement allows the publisher to pay you a lower amount per book sold, where the books are sold at a discount. If you are editing a book with chapters contributed by others, the publishing house may pay the chapter authors a small fee on publication. The total of these fees may then be set against your royalties.

Copyright may be held by the publisher or the author. In practice, this may make little difference as, in any case, the publisher will normally reserve exclusive publishing rights. In other cases the small print on contacts can be important. For instance, I would never sign a contract that gave the publisher an option on subsequent books.

Your contract is likely to say that the publisher reserves the right not to publish your book if you deliver it after a fixed date or if it is of poor quality. In practice, these clauses are not often invoked. Provided you have let your editor know in advance of the deadline, she or he will usually be willing to allow some slippage. On the other hand, you should not rely on this, as such slippage often causes the editor difficulties and may make it less likely that he or she will look favourably on your next proposal. If the book does not come up to expectations, she or he will also usually help you to improve it, rather than abandon it altogether. There will usually be a clause in the contract about excess correction charges.

It is in your interests to undertake careful proof-reading at the early stages. Once the book has been typeset, substantial changes late in the process can have knock-on effects you may not have anticipated: for instance, the indexing may need to be redone. Do not forget to check the spelling on the title pages. I have heard of a spelling mistake that was found on the cover after binding. As a consequence, the author lost several hundred pounds in royalties.

One decision you will have to make is whether to do your own indexing. Most publishers have links with professional indexers who will do this job for you for a charge that is set against royalties. Professional indexers usually do a sound job, but they may not know the subject area as well you do. If you decide to do your own index, your editor should be able to provide you with guidelines on the house-style and give you tips to make the job relatively painless (for instance, using a highlighter on a photocopy at the proof-reading stage to mark significant words and phrases). Indexing computer programs exist that can simplify the job a little.

Your relationship with your editor is likely to develop over time. Many authors stick with one editor for a considerable period. This relationship will be much easier if you are the sort of person who meets deadlines. Your editor is more likely to work hard on behalf of a cooperative and efficient author who answers correspondence promptly and delivers on time. Because the unexpected always occurs, I aim to complete the book well before the agreed deadline.

Good time management requires planning from the start. It may be useful to audit your position, to look at your commitments and decide what it is possible to do and to allow some leeway in your schedule. I am always disconcerted by the amount of time finishing a book takes (checking references, tidying headings, creating the table of contents and so on.) When you submit the manuscript, you need to be prepared for more work. The publisher may send you a marked-up manuscript to check before typesetting. If so, it is important that you have set aside the time to do a thorough job. This will be the last chance to make substantial changes. After the manuscript has been typeset, you may be asked to undertake thorough and careful proof-reading. At the same time, it is likely that you will be approached by the marketing department with requests for a range of information to help the publisher to sell the book. This is an important stage, and one to which you should give time and thought. It is probably a good idea to talk through the post-submission schedule with your publisher, so that you can blank out some days in your diary to do all this work.

The marketing of your book is partially your responsibility. The low profit margin on academic books means that your book is unlikely to be advertised in the press (unless it is part of a series that may be included in a composite advertisement). A few books will be sent out for review. If you expect to see your book described in the educational press during the following months, you may be disappointed. Not all books sent for review will be included and, even where they are, the review may not be printed for up to a year. Much marketing takes place through direct mail shots. The publicity department will need your help in targeting these. Another important marketing outlet is the conference circuit. You will need to inform the marketing department of key events where publicity about your book should be available. If you are giving a paper at a conference, you should make sure that you book is on prominent display. Do not be afraid to act as a shameless self-publicist.

Writing for a Journal

The most usual way of getting started in publishing is to write for a newspaper or journal. If you submit articles for the educational press, you will be up against stiff competition from professional journalists. Unless you have already established a name within education, you may find it is a difficult field to break into. You may be more likely to succeed if your article has something special that will catch the editor's attention. This 'something' may be topicality, controversy or human interest. If your area of enquiry has started to feature as a national issue (for example, the educational standards of students entering higher education), it is worth submitting a timely article to the educational press. If what you want to say is of direct application or relevance to the reader (for instance, induction programmes that minimize student drop-out), it may be publishable. On the whole, the educational press wants interesting articles, written in a short and non-technical way. It may not be interested in straightforward research reports.

Journals are likely to be more interested in the sort of research and enquiry that we have been suggesting in this series. You are unlikely to be paid for a paper or article in a journal, but this form of publishing can make a good starting point for a would-be academic author. Once you have completed your thinking, reading, research and/or enquiry, ideally you should consider the journals that might accept it before you start writing so that you can adapt your style to their requirements. I must admit that I have never taken this advice. I always write what I want to say, in my own style, and then look round for a journal that seems as if it might welcome that sort of paper. Whatever approach you take, you need to be aware that different journals carry various amounts of prestige in the world of education. This status is not an objective thing and is best ascertained by asking around your colleagues and fellow academic writers.

On the whole, you will achieve more status and professional recognition if you publish in a refereed journal, especially if it reaches an international audience. The refereeing process means that the quality of your paper is subjected to scrutiny by (usually two) outside experts, before it is published. They will often suggest that you should change your paper in various ways. You may want to consider these requests very seriously, since they are usually made by people who know a great deal about the subject and about writing. On the other hand, the paper is yours, and you may decide not to agree to changes if they would make the paper say things that you disagree with or change the tone you wish to take.

More status is accorded to publication in very well established journals. On the other hand, they tend to have a large number of experienced writers who regularly write for them: your paper will compete for space with many experts. You may stand a better chance of being published if you submit to a relatively new publication. My first paper appeared in the (then) new international journal *Assessment and Evaluation in Higher Education* that has now grown into a very well respected publication. If you start with a new journal, and if you both do well, you can build a long-lasting relationship to your mutual benefit.

The frequency of publication may be another factor in your choice of journal. Journals that only appear once or twice a year may not deal with your paper expeditiously. Since it is generally not 'done' to send your paper to several journals at the same time, this can be a real problem. A journal that publishes more regularly will probably referee and publish your paper more quickly. This is especially important if your paper is on a topical theme.

You will find detailed guidance at the back of most journals on you how the editors need you to set out your manuscript, references and so on. It will generally explain the usual length of acceptable articles and the number of copies of the manuscript that must be sent. It is important to keep to these guidelines.

Finding your Voice

When you start writing you will need to find your own style. On the whole it may be better for inexperienced writers to keep their style serious but simple. It is tempting to try to sound more authoritative by a 'mock posh' or passive way of writing. This is usually a mistake. Straightforward reporting, using as little jargon and as few conditional clauses as is consistent with the complexity of your subject matter, will probably work best.

The unique selling point of your book will influence the register and style of your writing. If you are writing for a highly specialized readership, with a wealth of expert knowledge and experience of reading difficult texts, you may get away with a more dense and complex writing style. On the other hand, if you are writing for undergraduate students, or busy lecturers or teachers, simple English with short sentences and paragraphs may communicate better. You will need to avoid being pompous but also to take into account the fact that books are different from letters and newspaper articles, and need a slightly more formal style. Written language is quite different from verbal communication. 'Conversational' styles of writing can come across as patronizing or unintelligent. For this reason, it is hard to bring off jokes or rhetorical questions in academic writing.

Gradually, you should learn to recognize your strengths and weaknesses. This awareness builds painfully over time. One of my own particular faults is that I can be too didactic. I now look through my work for imperatives, such as 'ought', 'must' and 'should' to check that I would not be better to replace them with more tentative words, such as 'might' or 'may' that imply that the reader has some choice in interpreting what I am suggesting. I also ask a few colleagues to read through anything I am submitting for publication and to be as critical and demanding as possible. I find that I have to write and rewrite up to 20 times before everyone is satisfied.

Annotated List of Education Publishers

Below I have listed many of the major publishers which are interested in books and/or curriculum materials to support teaching and learning within colleges and universities:

Cassell, Wellington House, 125 Strand, London WC2R 0BB. Telephone: 0171 420 5555.

Cassell publishes books aimed at teachers and undergraduate and postgraduate students of education and at the general market. The books reflect the most recent research into education, psychology and related academic subjects. While being at the cutting edge, they should also be clearly written and accessible. They are frequently aimed at the international market, while covering the most up-to-date policy developments in the UK.

The most recent editorial strategy is to publish a series of high level books of debates that feature international scholars.

David Fulton, 2 Barbon Close, Great Ormond Street, London WC1N 3JX. Telephone: 0171 405 5656.

David Fulton specializes in publishing within education, with a focus towards teachers of students and children with profound and multiple learning difficulties. It also publishes much for initial teacher education. It is hoping to build from this very strong base a list that covers other issues in the college and university sector.

It mainly publishes books which, while grounded in current research or classroom practice, set out lessons and issues for people to use in their professional practice or in their studies. It does not publish research *per se,* nor publish exclusively for the academic community.

It is a good publishing firm for a new author, since it will provide a personal service that includes much support and encouragement. In addition, its average turn around time from manuscript to finished book is under five months.

Education Now, 113 Arundel Drive, Bramcote Hills, Nottingham NG9 3FQ.

Education Now is a non-profit-making research, writing and publishing company, a cooperative devoted to developing more flexible and alternative forms of education. Its agenda includes the full range of educational contexts for learning, including home-based education, small schooling, mini-schooling, flexitime arrangements, democratic schooling and flexi-colleges. Underpinning this agenda is an emphasis on personalized education and learner-managed learning both within and outside the state education system.

Authors wishing to discuss a proposal for publication should first contact John Siraj-Blatchford at the University of Durham School of Education.

GETTING PUBLISHED

Falmer Press, 1 Gunpowder Square, London EC4A 3DE. Telephone: 0171 583 0490.

Falmer is a large and prestigious educational publisher. Once it has accepted your proposal, it will allow you to get on with your writing with little interference. This has the advantage for experienced writers of allowing much freedom, but does require that you are disciplined and know what you are doing.

Its list covers a wide variety of age ranges and subjects within education, including books on adolescence, equal opportunities, curriculum, educational policy and management, the disciplines of education, subject teaching, teacher education and student learning. The books are authoritative and well researched and are aimed at students, practitioners and academics.

Framework Press, Parkfield, Greaves Road, Lancaster LA1 4TZ. Telephone: 01524 39602.

This is a small, specialist publisher that is particularly interested in interactive curriculum and development materials. Much of its output is in the form of student-centred, activity-based material, in a ring-bound, photocopiable format (although it occasionally publishes books). The audience that it caters for includes students, teachers and educational managers. The list covers school and college management; staff development within schools, colleges and universities; vocational material, especially related to GNVQ; and curriculum material for English and Personal Social Education. The commissioning editor is interested in material covering all aspects of teaching and teaching methods. If you are interested in creating materials that will allow your readership to interact and to do things, rather than to take away and read, this may be the outlet for you.

Further Education Development Agency, Publications Department, Coombe Lodge, Blagdon, Bristol BS18 6RG. Telephone: 01761 462503.

This new agency is developing a publication list that will cover a variety of aspects of teaching, learning, assessment and management focusing particularly on the further education sector.

Heinemann, Halley Court, Jordan Hill, Oxford OX2 8EJ. Telephone: 01865 311366.

Heinemann is one of the major educational publishers. Its list covers a wide variety of aspects of teaching in the university and college sector.

Hodder and Stoughton, 338 Euston Road, London NW1 3BH. Telephone: 0171 873 6000.

Hodder and Stoughton Educational covers a wide range of subjects for further and higher education, including business, health and caring, catering, beauty therapy and vocational languages. At the higher education level, it has a teacher education list with a strongly practical focus, some of which is published in cooperation with the Open University.

Most of its publishing is taken up with core and supplementary textbooks, supported by teacher packs and student-centred workbooks. Its language publishing is fully supported by audio packs, with prize-winning CD-ROMs accompanying some courses.

Jessica Kingsley, 116 Pentonville Road, London N1 9JB. Telephone: 0171 833 2307.
Jessica Kingsley publishes books mainly for professionals. It asks authors to bear in mind that the essence of the sort of publishing that it does is that it should be a combination of theory and practice.

In the educational field, at school level they specialize in special educational needs, pastoral care and educational psychology. At further and higher education level, it publishes a series of books on management and policy. These include books on broad issues, such as quality in further education, and books with a narrower focus, such as the use of information technology in education management.

Kogan Page, 120 Pentonville Road, London N1 9JN. Telephone: 0171 278 0433.
Kogan Page is a large and well-respected publisher. It is always looking for book proposals in management and leadership, initial teacher education, mentoring, open and distance learning, learning theory, vocational education, research and assessment. It is always prepared to look at new areas if the proposal is good. The further and higher education commissioning editor points out that authors who follow the Kogan Page guidelines and do the background research are more likely to get a positive response or at least constructive criticism which will help develop the book. She also points out that many people do not do the background research to find out if a publisher is interested in a particular area and this accounts for a large number of rejections.

Macmillan, Brunel Road, Houndsmills, Basingstoke RG21 2XS. Telephone: 01256 29242.
Macmillan does not publish extensively in the field of education. It does however publish a range of study skills books for students.

Multilingual Matters, Frankfurt Lodge, Clevedon Hall, Victoria Road, Clevedon BS21 7SJ. Telephone: 01275 876519.
It specializes in books related to multicultural and anti-racist education.

Nelson, Nelson House, Mayfield Road, Walton-on-Thames, Surrey KT12 5PL. Telephone: 0932 246133.
It publishes post-16 curriculum textbooks.

Open University Press, Celtic Court, 22 Ballmoor, Buckingham MK18 1XW. Telephone: 01280 823388.
Open University Press publishes a range of books in conjunction with the Society for Research into Higher Education for academics world-wide in their generic professional roles as teachers, researchers and managers. It

currently publishes books in four fields (which can and do overlap):
planning and management; teaching, counselling and learning; history
and philosophy; and policy and context. The Press is particularly
interested in an international audience.

Authors are invited to apply to John Skelton at the Open University
Press for a book proposal guide.

Oxford University Press, Walton Street, Oxford OX2 6DP. Telephone: 01856
56767.
Oxford University Press does not specialize in education, but it is
interested in books in the area of political and social studies, especially
books for students, including undergraduate and postgraduate students
of education. These books tend to be related to the disciplines of
education (for instance, psychology and sociology). It also has a
management list for academics and would be interested in books in the
area of educational management and for the general public.

It has no standard format for book proposals.

Pergamon Press, Elsevier Science Ltd, The Boulevard, Langford Lane,
Kidlington OX5 1GB. Telephone: 01865 843000.
Pergamon Press has a small education list. It is currently interested in
books covering issues in higher education. These books tend to be
authoritative contributions to controversies in higher education, written
from a cross-national point of view. Studies in the series are each based on
comparisons between at least two countries. The intended audience
includes educational managers, administrators, teachers, researchers and
students.

Prospective authors are invited to contact Professor Guy Neave,
International Association of Universities.

Routledge, 11 New Fetter Lane, London EC4P 4EE. Telephone: 0171 583
9855.
Routledge has an extensive educational list that includes educational
management, teaching students with special educational needs and open
and distance learning. Its list covers all aspects of teaching and learning,
further and higher education, and the disciplines in education.

Scottish Academic Press, 56 Hanover Street, Edinburgh EH2 2DX. Telephone:
0131 255 7483.
Scottish Academic Press publishes a range of books on education, mostly
with a Scottish flavour. It aims to publish scholarly works in every field of
study and research. Its list covers the full age range and includes books on
assessment, subject teaching, curriculum development, management
issues, educational policy, comparative education, Scottish educational
history, student learning and teacher education.

Staff and Educational Development Association, Gala House, 3 Raglan Road,
Edgbaston, Birmingham B57 RA. Telephone: 0121 4405021.

The Association publishes SEDA Papers in the form of short A4 books and is also cooperating with Kogan Page to produce a series of books on teaching in universities.

SEDA Papers are published for a mainly UK audience and may be edited collections or authored books. You will not have to provide an index, and you should use accessible language. The Papers tend to be published in small print runs and you will not receive royalties or expenses.

The book series contains books of around 60,000 words, written for an international audience. They may be edited collections or authored books. Again, royalties go to SEDA.

Sally Brown, Educational Development Service, University of Northumbria at Newcastle, Newcastle upon Tyne NE1 8ST, Telephone 0191 227 3985, will be happy to talk to you informally about your proposal or to send you guidelines for authors.

Technical and Educational Services, Ravenswood Road, Bristol BS6 6BW.
It has a small list, mainly by the same group of authors focused on helpful hints for higher education teachers.

Trentham Books, Westview House, 734 London Road, Oakhill, Stoke on Trent, Staffs ST4 5NP. Telephone: 01782 745567.
Trentham Books publishes about 25 titles each year and is keen to encourage new and inexperienced educational authors. Many of its books focus on work with traditionally disadvantaged groups, including ethnic, linguistic and religious minorities. Its current catalogue also includes books on early years education, educational management, and design and technology education. Trentham publishes promptly and is able to turn a manuscript into a published book within two or three months.

Prospective authors should contact Gillian Klein at the editorial office, 28 Hillside Gardens, London N6 5ST, Telephone 0181 348 2174.

Annotated List of Education Journals

The list of journals below includes the name of the journal, the publisher, the frequency of publication and the name and address of the editor(s) to whom material for publication should be sent. These details were sent to me by the publishers at the time of writing, but, since editors can move on and (less frequently) editorial policies can change, you might be wise to check them before you embark on publication. Most of the journals will also accept book reviews, shorter discussion papers and research summaries.

Disability and Society
Carfax. Published quarterly.

Manuscripts to: L Barton, Division of Education, University of Sheffield, 388 Glossop Road, Sheffield S10 2AJ.
This refereed journal takes its international readership seriously. It does not state its editorial policy. Education features strongly within the journal, but it also draws on disciplines across the humanities, behavioural and social sciences. Papers are highly eclectic and include empirical research, historical and cultural analysis and project evaluation.

Gender and Education

Carfax. Published three times a year.
Manuscripts to: C Hughes, Department of Continuing Education, University of Warwick, Coventry CV4 7AL.
This international, refereed journal publishes short 'polemics' as well as more traditional papers. It is interested in feminist knowledge, theory, consciousness, action and debate. Much of the research published within it is in the qualitative tradition. In Volume 7, Number 1, there is an editorial that gives a detailed account of how the editors would like to see the journal developing; this includes a continuation of the previous tradition, but also more quantitative research, longitudinal studies about the methodological debate, and comparative and international perspectives, including issues of race.

Innovation and Learning in Education: The International Journal for the Reflective Practitioner

MCB University Press, Published three times a year.
Manuscripts to: G McElwee, School of Management, University of Humberside, Cottingham Road, Hull HU6 7RT.
This is a new journal that is committed to a critical evaluation of teaching, learning and related issues in post-compulsory education. It is looking for papers that bridge the gap between theory and practice, and as such it is a good vehicle for the kind of insider research that is located within a theoretical framework. It is particularly interested in exploring the ways that teaching and learning may be enhanced within a context of reducing resources. It seeks to share good practice, stimulate and encourage debate and enhance teaching and learning. It is looking for papers from a variety of 'insiders': teachers, course leaders, managers and others. Papers tend to be short (up to 3,000 words). They are often broken up by sub-headings and diagrams. The language of the papers tends to be fairly non-academic and reader-friendly.

Innovations in Education and Training International

Kogan Page, Published quarterly.
Manuscripts to: Philip Barker, School of Computing and Mathematics, The University of Teesside, Cleveland TS1 3BA.
This journal is a relaunch of *Education and Training Technology International*. It is interested in papers that would help practitioners and managers keep abreast of innovations and update their skills. It publishes

refereed papers, case studies and papers based on opinion. The important criterion is that material submitted should reflect the state-of-the-art in education and training. The journal is published in cooperation with major UK staff development associations and reflects their priority of direct application to practice. This makes it a particularly appropriate vehicle for insider research, especially if it involves the uses of technology.

Journal of Access Studies

Jessica Kingsley, Published twice a year.

Manuscripts to: P Jones, Higher Education Quality Council.

This journal aims to be the authoritative voice for Access studies. It is written for practitioners and teaching staff, but also for managers, policy-makers and education guidance workers. It includes refereed articles, project reports and shorter (often polemical) contributions on current issues and debates. The focus is on routes into higher education, strategies of training and employment, collaborative mechanisms to support Access and the impact of Access on the policy and practice of universities.

Mentoring and Tutoring for Partnership in Learning

Trentham Books. Published three times a year.

Manuscripts to: J Egglestone, c/o Trentham Books Ltd, Westview Road, 734 London Road, Oakhill, Stoke on Trent ST4 5NP.

This international journal gives little guidance to authors. It seems to be interested in papers on mentoring and tutoring in a wide variety of contexts. The tone of the papers, which is practical and non-technical, suggests an audience that includes newcomers to this work. The papers seem to be mainly concerned with 'how to' guides to practice, reports of small-scale research and project evaluation and the discussion of issues.

Multicultural Teaching to Combat Racism in School and Community

Trentham. Published three times a year.

Manuscripts to: G Klein, Department of Education, University of Warwick, Coventry CV4 7AL.

This journal covers all aspects of teaching and learning in a multicultural society. It is particularly interested in papers about inter-professional work, professional practice, the discussion of aims and purposes and reports of evaluation projects. It contains short papers that are not academic in tone. This might be a good outlet for reports of the evaluation of innovation or insider research.

Pastoral Care in Education

Blackwells, Published six times a year.

Manuscripts to: R Best, Froebel Institute College, Grove House, Roehampton Lane, London SW15 5PJ.

This journal is concerned with all aspects of pastoral care in any educational setting. The papers include critical analysis of new and existing practice. programmes and methods, discussion of controversial issues as well as traditional research reports. The articles are very varied in length. The journal welcomes new authors.

Studies in the Education of Adults
National Institution of Adult and Continuing Education. Published twice a year.
Manuscripts to: J Wallis, Department of Educational Studies, University of Nottingham NG7 2RD.
This established refereed journal is addressed to academic specialists, practitioners and managers who wish to keep abreast of scholarship, theory-building and empirical research. The tone of the papers tends to be technical and highly academic. The papers reflect the critical debate of contemporary issues and are located in a thorough understanding of the relevant literature.

Other Journals

You may be interested in publishing in some of the journals listed below. The editorial policy of some of them are described in Ashcroft and Palacio (1996), Bennett *et al.* (1996) or Higgins *et al.* (1996).

Assessment and Evaluation in Higher Education
Carfax. Published three times a year.
Manuscripts to: WAH Scott, School of Education, University of Bath.

Assessment in Education: Principles, Policy and Practice
Carfax. Published three times a year.
Manuscripts to: P Broadfoot, School of Education, University of Bristol.

Association for Learning Technology Journal
Association for Learning Technology. Published twice a year.
Manuscripts to: G Jacob, University College, Swansea.

British Educational Research Journal
Carfax. Published quarterly.
Manuscripts to: G Weiner, Department of Education, South Bank Polytechnic, London.

British Journal of Educational Psychology
British Psychological Society. Published quarterly.
Manuscripts to: M Youngman, University of Nottingham.

British Journal of Educational Studies
Blackwell. Published quarterly.
Manuscripts to: D Halpin, Institute of Education, University of Warwick, Coventry.

British Journal of In-Service Education
   Triangle. Published three times a year.
   Manuscripts to: M Lee, University College of Bretton Hall, Wakefield.

British Journal of Music Education
   Cambridge University Press. Published three times a year.
   Manuscripts to: J Paynter, University of York, or K Swanwick, University of
   London Institute of Education.

British Journal of Religious Education
   Alden Press. Published three times a year.
   Manuscripts to: JM Hall, University of Birmingham.

British Journal of Sociology of Education
   Carfax. Published quarterly.
   Manuscripts to: L Barton, Division of Education, University of Sheffield.

Cambridge Journal of Education
   Triangle. Published three times a year.
   Manuscripts to: B Shannon, University of Cambridge Institute of
   Education.

Comparative Education
   Carfax. Published three times a year.
   Manuscripts to: P Broadfoot, University of Bristol.

Compare: A Journal of Comparative Education
   Carfax. Published three times a year.
   Manuscripts to: C Brock, University of Oxford.

Computers and Education
   Pergamon. Published eight times a year.
   Manuscripts to: MR Kibby, University of Strathclyde.

Curriculum Inquiry
   Blackwell. Published quarterly.
   Manuscripts to: FM Connolly, The Ontario Institute for Studies in
   Education, Canada.

The Curriculum Journal
   Routledge. Published three times a year.
   Manuscripts to: M James, University of Cambridge Institute of Education.

Curriculum Studies
   Triangle. Published three times a year.
   Manuscripts to: W Carr, Division of Education, University of Sheffield.

Education Economics
   Carfax. Published three times a year.
   Manuscripts to: G Johnes, Lancaster University.

Education Today
Pitman. Published quarterly.
Manuscripts to: The Editor, College of Preceptors, Coppice Row, Theydon Bois, Epping.

Educational Action Research
Triangle. Published three times a year.
Manuscripts to: Dr B Somekh, University of East Anglia, Norwich.

Educational Management and Administration
Pitman. Published quarterly.
Manuscripts to: P Ribbins, University of Birmingham.

Educational Psychology
Carfax. Published quarterly.
Manuscripts to: R Riding, University of Birmingham.

Educational Research
Routledge. Published three time a year
Manuscripts to: S Hegarty, National Foundation for Educational Research, Slough.

Educational Review
Carfax. Published three times a year.
Manuscripts to: The Editors, School of Education, University of Birmingham.

Educational Studies
Carfax. Published three times a year.
Manuscripts to: D Cherrington, International Centre for Advanced Studies, Cheltenham and Gloucester College of Higher Education.

Educational Studies in Mathematics
Kluwer Academic Publishers. Published four times a year.
Manuscripts to: Kluwer Academic Publishers, Dordrecht, The Netherlands.

Educational Theory
University of Illinois. Published four times a year.
Manuscripts to: NC Burbules, University of Illinois, USA.

Environmental Education Research
Carfax. Published three times a year.
Manuscripts to: C Oulton, University of Bath.

European Journal of Education
Carfax. Published quarterly.
Manuscripts to: The Editors, European Institute of Education and Social Policy, Universite de Paris.

European Journal of Engineering Education
   Carfax. Published quarterly.
   Manuscripts to: T Becher, University of Sussex.

European Journal of Special Needs
   Routledge. Published three times a year.
   Manuscripts to: S Hegarty, National Foundation for Educational
   Research, Slough.

European Journal of Teacher Education
   Carfax. Published three times a year.
   Manuscripts to: M Todeschini, Istituto di Pedagogia, Universita degli
   studii, Milan, Italy.

Evaluation and Research in Education
   Multilingual Matters. Published three times a year.
   Manuscripts to: K Morrison, School of Education, University of Durham.

Evaluation Practice
   JAI Press. Published three times a year.
   Manuscripts to: M Smith, 2115 Symons Hall, University of Maryland,
   College Park, USA.

Forum for Promoting 3–19 Comprehensive Education
   Triangle. Published three times a year.
   Manuscripts to: N Whitbread, Beaumont Cottage, East Langton, Market
   Harborough.

Higher Education Policy
   Kogan Page. Published quarterly.
   Manuscripts to: International Association of Universities, Unesco House,
   1 rue Miollis, 75732 Paris Cedex 15, France.

Higher Education Quarterly
   Blackwells. Published quarterly.
   Manuscripts to: M Shattock, Senate House, University of Warwick, Coventry.

Higher Education Review
   Tyrrell Burgess Associates. Published three times a year.
   Manuscripts to: J Pratt, 46 Merers Road, London.

Interchange
   Kluwer Academic Press. Published three times a year.
   Manuscripts to: L Lenz, Faculty of Education, University of Calgary, 2500
   University Drive NW, Toronto, Ontario, Canada.

International Journal of Disability and Development in Education
   University of Queensland Press. Published three times a year.
   Manuscripts to: F and E Schonell, Special Education Centre, St Lucia,
   Australia.

GETTING PUBLISHED

International Journal of Education Research
Pergamon Press. Published 12 times a year.
Manuscripts to: HJ Walberg, University of Illinois, Chicago, USA.

International Journal of Science Education
Taylor and Francis. Published six times a year.
Manuscripts to: JK Gilbert, University of Reading.

International Journal of Technology and Design Education
Kluwer Academic Press. Published three times a year.
Manuscripts to: The Editor, Kluwer Academic Publishers, Dordrecht, The
Netherlands.

International Research in Geographical and Environmental Education
La Trobe University Press. Published twice a year.
Manuscripts to: J Lidstone, Queensland University of Technology,
Australia.

International Studies in Sociology of Education
Triangle. Published twice a year.
Manuscripts to: L Barton, Division of Education, University of Sheffield.

Journal for Educational Policy
Taylor and Francis. Published six times a year.
Manuscripts to: S Ball, Kings College, London.

Journal of Aesthetic Education
University of Illinois Press. Published quarterly.
Manuscripts to: University of Illinois, USA.

Journal of Art and Design Education
Blackwell. Published three times a year.
Manuscripts to: J Swift, University of Central England, Birmingham.

Journal of Biological Education
Institute of Biology. Published quarterly.
Manuscripts to: The Editor, Institute of Biology, London.

Journal of Computer Assisted Learning
Blackwell. Published quarterly.
Manuscripts to: R Lewis, University of Lancaster.

Journal of Education for Teaching
Carfax. Published three times a year.
Manuscripts to: E Stones, 11 Serpentine Road, Selly Park, Birmingham.

Journal of Educational Television
Carfax. Published three times a year.
Manuscripts to: M Messenger Davies, The London Institute.

Journal of Further and Higher Education
NATFHE. Published three times a year.
Manuscripts to: A Castling, c/o NATFHE, London.

Journal of Geography in Higher Education
Carfax. Published three times a year.
Manuscripts to: M Healey, Cheltenham and Gloucester College of Higher Education.

Journal of Information Technology for Teacher Education
Triangle. Published three times a year.
Manuscripts to: B Robinson, Department of Education, University of Cambridge.

Journal of Moral Education
Carfax. Published three times a year.
Manuscripts to: MJ Taylor, National Foundation for Educational Research.

Journal of Open and Distance Learning
Open University/ Pitman. Published three times a year.
Manuscripts to: J Matthews, Regional Academic Services, The Open University, Milton Keynes.

Journal of Philosophy of Education
Redwood Books. Published three times a year.
Manuscripts to: R Smith, University of Durham.

Journal of Teacher Development
Pitman. Published quarterly.
Manuscripts to: M Golby, School of Education, University of Exeter.

Management in Education
Pitman. Published quarterly.
Manuscripts to: The Editor, Putteridge Bury, University of Luton.

Medical Teacher
Carfax. Published quarterly.
Manuscripts to: RM Harden, Ninewells Hospital and Medical School.

New Academic
SEDA. Published three times a year.
Manuscripts to: E Mapstone, St Yse, St Nectan's Glen, Tintagel, Cornwall.

Oxford Review of Education
Carfax. Published three times a year.
Manuscripts to: D Phillips, University of Oxford Department of Educational Studies.

Physics Education
Institute of Physics Publishing. Published three times a year.
Manuscripts to: Institute of Physics, Bristol.

Qualitative Studies in Education
  Taylor and Francis. Published four times a year.
  Manuscripts to: S Ball, Centre for Educational Studies, King's College London.

Quality Assurance in Education
  MCB University Press. Published three times a year.
  Manuscripts to: G McElwee, School of Management, University of Humberside, Hull.

Quality in Higher Education
  Carfax. Published three times a year.
  Manuscripts to: L Harvey, University of Central England, Birmingham.

Research in Drama Education
  Carfax. Published quarterly.
  Manuscripts to: J Somers, University of Exeter.

Research into Science and Technological Education
  Carfax. Published twice a year.
  Manuscripts to: CR Brown, University of Hull.

Research Papers in Education
  Routledge. Published three times a year.
  Manuscripts to: P Preece, School of Education, University of Exeter.

Sport, Education and Society
  Carfax. Published quarterly.
  Manuscripts to: C Hardy, University of Loughborough.

Studies in Educational Evaluation
  Pergamon. Published quarterly.
  Manuscripts to: A Lewy, School of Education, Tel Aviv University; M Alkin, Graduate School of Education, UCLA, Los Angeles; B McGaw, Australian Council of Educational Research, Victoria, Australia; or R Langeheine, Institute for Science Education (IPN), University of Kiel, Germany.

Studies in Higher Education
  Society for Research into Higher Education/Carfax. Published quarterly.
  Manuscripts to: R Barnett, Institute of Education, London.

Teachers and Teaching: Theory and Practice
  Carfax. Published three times a year.
  Manuscripts to: C Day, ISATT, University of Nottingham.

Teaching and Teacher Education
  Pergamon Press. Published six times a year.
  Manuscripts to: N Bennett, University of Exeter.

Teaching in Higher Education
Carfax. Published three times a year.
Manuscripts to: L Barton, Division of Education, University of Sheffield.

Tertiary Education and Management
Jessica Kingsley. Published twice a year.
Manuscripts to: NR Begg, The University of Aberdeen.

The Vocational Aspects of Education
Triangle. Published three times a year.
Manuscripts to: B Bailey, University of Greenwich, London.

Westminster Studies in Education
Carfax. Published annually.
Manuscripts to: WF Fearon, Westminster College, Oxford.

Annotated Reading List

American Psychological Association (1983) *Publication Manual of the American Psychological Association* (3rd edn), Washington, DC: American Psychological Association.
A guide to the style for formal research papers required by a number of international journals.

Cave, R and Cave, J (1985) *Writing for Promotion and Profit: A guide to educational publishing*. Newmarket: Ron and Joyce Cave Educational Consultants.
A short, rather over-simplified manual that concentrates on facts rather than skills and provides some useful tips on getting published. It may help you to understand the contract, once you receive it.

Berry, R (1986) *How to Write a Research Paper*, Oxford: Pergamon.
A short book that covers a number of technical aspects, such as preparing a bibliography and dealing with footnotes, that I have not had space to cover in this chapter. Worth reading if you are new to publishing and lack a source of expert advice.

Open University (1993) *An Equal Opportunities Guide to Language and Image*, Buckingham: Open University Press.
Many publishers have guides to inclusive language. If yours does not, it is essential that you are aware of the hidden messages that your use of language may convey. The Open University guide is very short (19 pages) and is simple and user-friendly.

Collected Original Sources in Education, Oxford: Carfax.
A microfiche journal dealing with original international educational research in full.

The following journals, all published by Carfax, provide summaries of many hundred journals, articles and/or books published across the world each year. They are a useful means of identifying the most up-to-date research and debate in particular areas of enquiry within education:

Content Pages in Education
Educational Technology
Higher Education Abstracts
Multicultural Education Abstracts
Research into Higher Education Abstracts
Sociology of Education Abstracts
Special Educational Needs Abstracts
Technical Education and Training Abstracts.

References

Ashcroft, K and Palacio, D (1996) *Researching into Assessment and Evaluation in Colleges and Universities*, London: Kogan Page.
Bennett, C, Higgins, C and Foreman-Peck, L (1996) *Researching into Teaching Methods in Colleges and Universities*, London: Kogan Page.
Higgins, C, Reading J and Taylor, P (1996) *Researching into Learning Resources in Colleges and Universities*, London: Kogan Page.

Acknowledgements

I am particularly grateful to John Owens of David Fulton Publishers for much of the background information about the publisher's perspective that is included in this chapter.

I would like to thank Peter Knight of SEDA, Naomi Roth of Cassell Publishers, Oxford University Press, John Skelton of Open University Press, Liz Cartell of Framework Press, Elisabeth Tribe of Hodder and Stoughton Educational, Pat Lomax of Kogan Page, and Jessica Kingsley for their willingness to give up their time to provide me with the information to make this section as useful to the reader as possible.

Index